UP
TO
SPEED

SECRETS OF
REDUCING TIME
TO
PROFICIENCY

STEVE ROSENBAUM
AUTHOR OF *LEARNING PATHS*

UP TO SPEED: *Secrets of Reducing Time to Proficiency*
Copyright © 2018 by Steve Rosenbaum

ISBN (Print Edition): 978-1-54392-925-6
ISBN (eBook Edition): 978-1-54392-926-3

CONTENTS

Foreword

I first became acquainted with Steve Rosenbaum's work shortly after the first publication of our own book *The Six Disciplines of Breakthrough Learning*. The *Six Disciplines* was the result of our effort to understand why some companies get so much better results from learning and development than others. The secret, we found, was in focusing on business needs and treating training as a process, rather than in chasing the latest trend or having the most "gee-whiz" technology.

When I met Steve and learned more about the Learning Paths methodology, I knew I had found a kindred spirit: someone with a pragmatic approach and fresh ideas for getting greater business value from investments in training and development. In the years since, I have had many long conversations with Steve (those who know him, know such conversations are rarely short) about the opportunities for making training much more effective and valuable.

I have benefited greatly from his insights, humor, wisdom, and deep experience—the result of implementing Learning Paths across a wide range of industries, jobs, and geographies. Now, in this long-awaited sequel to the original *Learning Paths* book, Steve distills that wisdom and shares the lessons he has gleaned from another dozen years of experience.

The pivotal insight of Learning Paths is, as its name implies, the recognition that there is a pathway from novice to journeyman, from an unskilled to a proficient performer. Getting to competence is a *journey;* it cannot be accomplished in a single leap or as the result of a few-day or even a few-week training program. Proficiency develops over time, through multiple learning experiences, practice, and feedback.

As with any journey, some routes are more efficient than others. Some are direct; others are tortuous with needless delays and detours. Some paths are well-marked with clear milestones; others are unmarked and hopelessly confusing so that you never know where you are. The job of corporate learning professionals is to help define, design, implement, and manage the optimal pathway to enable employees to complete the journey to proficiency as quickly, efficiently, and consistently as possible.

Steve is adamant that training professionals need to be clear about what they fundamentally believe about learning since that determines how they approach their jobs. Once, when we were making a joint presentation at the Association for Talent Development, Steve began the seminar by asking: "What do you truly believe to be true about learning?" We were greeted by blank looks. Apparently, few had ever thought deeply about the question. In this new edition of *Learning Paths,* he suggests some principles to consider.

One is that knowing is not the same as doing. Although he began his career as an instructional designer, well-steeped in ADDIE and learning objectives, Steve has never lost sight of the real *raison d'être* of corporate learning: to help the business achieve its objectives. To accomplish business goals, employees need to *do* their jobs competently, safely, and well; it is not enough that they know *how.* Value is created by *doing* rather than just *knowing.* Thus, the Learning Paths approach focuses on what employees need to *do* and the best and most efficient way for them to learn that.

A well-designed learning path includes *all* the learning experiences that an employee needs to perform his or her job competently. Unfortunately, most organizations still approach training as a "one-and-done" training event, in which the end of the class is the end of the journey. Some years ago, I was an invited instructor at one of the most famous corporate leadership development centers. Over dinner, I asked a group of participants in the Management Development Program, "What are you expected to do with what you have learned when you return to work?" They looked at me as if I had two heads. "Do?" they asked. It never occurred to them that they were expected to *do* anything afterward. The path (and the learning) dead-ended at the classroom door. In contrast, a proper Learning Path leads all the way to the destination: competent on-the-job performance.

The Learning Paths approach is not about training philosophy; it's about business results. A well-designed learning path shortens the time before an employee becomes a net contributor, rather than a net cost, to the organization. It also generates significant savings in recruiting and onboarding costs; employees who are more productive more quickly are more likely to stay with the organization. In a large organization, an effective learning path—as opposed to traditional onboarding approaches—can save millions of dollars.

The second key principle of Learning Paths is that learning how to do a job should occur by design, not by accident. Given the very real costs and risks associated with incompetent performance, it is a mistake to simply hope that employees will pick up critical skills on the job or by osmosis. There is simply too much variability in what they experience. And variability, as the great quality guru, W. Edwards Deming, taught us, is the enemy of quality. Saying that learning should occur by design, is not to say by any means, that all skills require classroom or computer-based training. Quite the contrary: on-the-job coaching, mentoring, and just-in-time learning are vital parts of any learning path. The point is that all the essential learning experiences need to be planned and executed with the same care and attention that has traditionally been lavished on classroom and e-learning events.

A final strength of the Learning Paths approach is its emphasis on continuous process improvement. No path is perfect and, as Will Rogers pointed out, "Even if you are on the right track, you will get run over if you just sit there." The application of process improvement philosophies and methodologies to manufacturing has resulted in higher-quality products at lower costs than at any time in history. Applying these same techniques to training and development likewise improves quality and reduces cost. Process improvement, however, depends on having a clear definition of the quality of the output and methods to measure it. Learning Paths provides the answers: quality from training is defined as the ability to perform independently to the required standard for a given job. The key metric is the time to achieve that level of performance ("time to Independence Day," as Steve like to call it). In the Learning Paths approach, the results of the current process are monitored, and opportunities to improve the process are proposed and implemented. The results are assessed, and further improvements are identified based on the results: a classic Deming PDCA Cycle.

Given that the benefits of implementing Learning Paths are documented, obvious, and compelling, why hasn't the approach been universally applied in corporate training and development? The main hurdle is our own mindset. For years, learning professionals and business leaders alike have seen the role of training as delivering *training*. As such, we have tracked, scored, reported, and rewarded the number of hours of training and whether people enjoyed it. In fact, the real job of training and development, as Steve points out, is to enhance employee performance, achieve business goals, and create competitive advantage. The company that does that most effectively and efficiently wins.

To enhance the stature and value of training, we need to embrace Learning Paths and reorient attention from achieving learning objectives to achieving performance objectives. Once a performance perspective is adopted, then it is clear that the responsibility for enhancing employee performance is shared by trainers and managers. The rest is relatively straightforward (although not necessarily easy). Steve provides the roadmap:

- Define what "proficiency" means for a given job
- Determine the time it typically takes for employees to become independently proficient in that role today
- Map the current learning path

- Re-engineer it to eliminate waste, gain speed, and improve quality of the output.

In this very readable book, you will find numerous examples of how to implement Learning Paths and the benefits of doing so. You will also find lots of practical advice that Steve has learned in the "School of Hard Knocks," working with real companies on real, complex, and critical training challenges. Redefining corporate learning as a journey and designing a learning path for the complete learning experience are the two most important steps learning professionals can take to increase their value and earn a meaningful seat at the management table.

So what are you waiting for?

Roy V.H. Pollock

Author of *The Six Disciplines of Breakthrough Learning*

Roy Pollock is the Chief Learning Officer and co-founder of the 6Ds Company. He is the co-author of the best-selling book *The Six Disciplines of Breakthrough Learning*, which explains the six practices the differentiate high-impact from low-impact training programs. Dr. Pollock is an international speaker and consultant who has a passion for helping individuals and organizations excel.

Before helping create the 6Ds Company, Dr. Pollock served as Chief Learning Officer for the Fort Hill Company; Assistant Dean for Curriculum Development, Cornell College of Veterinary Medicine; Vice President of the Companion Animal Division for Pfizer, and President of IDEXX informatics. Dr. Pollock received his B.A. *magna cum laude* from Williams College, his Doctor of Veterinary Medicine degree with highest honors as well as his Ph.D. from Cornell University. He lives and works at Swamp College in Trumansburg, New York.

Acknowledgments

Hundreds of people had a big input into this book. They were part of scores of projects, workshops, and webinars where all of the research, experience, and stories happened. I've always said that I learn something new every time I talk about Learning Paths.

One of my first clients in this business back in 1980 was Dr. Jim Lynn who taught me the expressions "Gestalt," "Right hemisphere probes," and "Reptilian brain." Jim's older brother was Mike Lynn, former general manager of the Minnesota Vikings. This led to an opportunity to ghostwrite a book on team building with Joe Kapp, former Vikings quarterback and Cal football coach.

Jim also introduced me to Ed Robbins back before GE bought Gelco. I've been doing work with Ed at every stop in his career from Gelco to Wilson Learning to GE Capital and to Ceridian. Ed is my go-to expert on leadership and change management. When Ed was in charge of the quality curriculum at Wilson Learning, he introduced me to Al Frank. Al is not only the smartest person I know in the training industry but also a master woodworker.

I remember that one of the first projects I worked on as a freelancer for Wilson Learning was for a medical device manufacturer. Between the client and Wilson Learning, 35 people were working on the project. By the time the project was over, I was the only person on either side who hadn't quit or was fired.

Around 1990, I started to work with Ira Kasdan on major projects in the travel industry. Ira also brought me into a lot of Learning Path projects in the insurance industry which continue even today. Ira is now mastering doing nothing as he spends each morning on the beach in Florida. Ira introduced me to Gloria Stock Mickelson who started at Carlson Wagonlit Travel and is now leading the training efforts at TravelLeaders. Gloria has always been my best client because she really gets training and is very open to new ideas and change.

Around 1995, I was introduced to Jim Williams when he was at GE Capital Transport International Pool. We did a few projects before Jim went off to India to lead the training efforts for GE Capital International Services. This association led to Jim being a coauthor on the *Learning Paths* book. Jim was key in making the connection between training and quality improvement. This strongly influenced how we treated learning as a process. Jim went on to take a senior leadership role at several other companies where we continued working on Learning Path projects together.

I also want to give special recognition to Nick Maras who held numerous high-level jobs in the Minnesota College system. Nick was instrumental in all of the grant work through Minnesota Job Skills. Yes, Nick is related to baseball legend Roger Maris. Nick and Roger's father worked on the railroad together in Hibbing, Minnesota.

After the publication of the *Learning Paths* book, I started to get a professional following of well-known thought leaders in the training industry. I'd like to give a special thanks to Roy Pollock who wrote the foreword to this book. I'd also like to thank Dr. Carl Binder for reviewing this book. Carl also gave me great insight into the concept of "Fluency." Finally, Ajay Pangarkar taught me several interesting concepts on how to tie training results to financial measures.

Three other key people have helped bring *Learning Paths* to an international audience. Chunlei Zhu brought *Learning Paths* to China and in the process has become a great friend. He has done a lot of innovation with *Learning Paths* and has become very successful.

Second, Cees Nieboer has been handling *Learning Paths* in Europe. He is a Dutch native living in Slovenia but speaks perfect English. He has been helping me edit this book almost daily.

The third is Lydia Cille-Schmidt who has done some remarkable projects with Learning Paths in South Africa. Lydia is always on top of all the latest trends in the training industry.

My technology guru is Marty Rosenheck. He is helping us bring Learning Path deliverables online using state-of-the-art practices. Marty is always pushing us to use the capabilities of emerging technology to improve compliance and learning transfer.

Steve Barone, a former senior executive in the insurance industry, is the newest member of the team. Steve is leading an effort to proliferate Learning Paths everywhere rapidly.

Now for the really important people. My wife Pamela has been along for the entire ride. She has urged me to write my books by writing two of her own. Her first book *Unlucky Star* about Hawaii's last princess was published in 2004 within months of the *Learning Paths*. Her second book, *A Barista Spills the Beans*, coming out in 2018, tells the tale of nine months working at Starbucks. My Parents, Dave and Joyce Rosenbaum now 97 and 90, provide years of stories that appear in this book.

Introduction

Up to Speed: Unlocking the Secrets of Reducing Time to Proficiency tells the story of working on Learning Paths initiatives over the last fifteen years since the publishing of the book *Learning Paths: Increase Profits by Reducing the Time It Takes to Get Employees Up-to-Speed.* The *Learning Paths* book has a lot of forms and templates that continue to make it a valuable tool for working on training projects.

The term "Up to Speed" means reaching a desired level of performance. Therefore, in the book, it's used as a synonym for proficiency. The faster any employee is up to speed, the better.

Chapter Previews

Here's a quick peek at the insides of this book. I've written a quick chapter by chapter description in case you want to skip around a little.

Chapter 1 – The Journey

This chapter describes the journey from the publication of the first Learning Paths book to present day. It's a story about how things have evolved and changed.

Chapter 2 – The Business Case

The starting point for any Learning Paths initiative is a sound business case. This chapter talks about using the concept of time to proficiency as the business case.

Chapter 3 – The Value of Learning Principles

Learning Paths is rooted in three learning principles or beliefs about how people really learn. The principles are reflected throughout the book.

Chapter 4 – Starting on the Same Page

The concepts of proficiency, time to proficiency, and a Learning Path are described in this chapter. It's designed to provide a common language that's used throughout the book.

Chapter 5 – Relying on Experts

This chapter discusses forming a team of experts and using their knowledge and expertise to drive a Learning Paths initiative.

Chapter 6 – Do You Know It When You See It?

This chapter focuses on how to identify, describe, and measure proficiency in order to drive rapid improvement. It presents the structure of a proficiency definition including identifying proficiency milestones.

Chapter 7 – A Process Approach to Learning

If learning is a process and not an event, then everything we know about process improvement can be applied to build great Learning Paths. This chapter focuses on how to drive out time, waste, and variability.

Chapter 8 – Sequence, Sequence, Sequence

This chapter talks about the demise of pick and choose learning and replaces it with a sequence of learning activities that the experts say works the best.

Chapter 9 – Getting Technology Right

Technology changes how people do their jobs. Without changing how we train these jobs, the technology training fails. This chapter presents ideas on how to integrate technology training on a Learning Path.

Chapter 10 – When Good Isn't Good Enough

75% isn't an acceptable passing score for most jobs. In fact, in some jobs, there can't be any mistakes such as landing a plane. This chapter presents ideas on how to evaluate training in a meaningful way and how to improve testing.

Chapter 11 – All Aboard

The first 30 to 90 days often determines an employee's long-term success. Onboarding is often part of a Learning Path. This chapter presents three key ideas on how to maximize onboarding.

Chapter 12 – Making Informal Training Formal

This chapter explores the principle that training should be by design and not by accident. It provides ideas on how to transform on-the-job and experiential learning into learning by design.

Chapter 13 – Making It "Stick"

This chapter describes a strategy for successfully implementing and maintaining a Learning Paths initiative. It focuses on the key principles of effective change management.

Chapter 14 – More for Less

Most organizations look at training as a cost rather than an expense. Therefore, getting the most out of every training dollar is critical. This chapter shows a Learning Paths approach to getting more for less.

Chapter 15 - The Sales Learning Path

This chapter explores ideas on how to develop salespeople through using a Learning Path. It discusses how traditional sales training is only one piece of a much larger puzzle. It's more than "what" salespeople need to know but "how" they are going to use it in real life situations.

Chapter 16 – The Leadership Path

The chapter is not about the qualities of a leader. It describes how to develop leaders at all levels of the organization. It applies the concepts and principles of Learning Paths to leaders.

Chapter 17 – Learning Paths in Schools

This chapter asks readers to stretch their imaginations to see how applying Learning Paths to schools could make a dramatic difference.

Chapter 18 – Getting it Together: Mergers, Acquisitions, Outsourcing, and Centralization

This chapter discusses that challenges of training across organizations as they merge, outsource and recombine.

Chapter 19 – What's the Association

This chapter presents ideas for applying Learning Paths to associations and other membership organizations that have thousands of members, eager for training.

Chapter 20 - Final Note

This chapter wraps up the key ideas presented in this book and looks ahead to the next ten years.

CHAPTER 1

The Journey

Before starting this journey, I want to define a couple of terms that will be used several hundred times in this book. These terms are often defined in many ways by many people. I have been trying to set a standard for these terms so that there is a common language.

The first term is proficiency. I define proficiency as a level of performance in terms of output, quality, speed, and safety. The concept of being up to speed directly relates to proficiency.

The second term is Learning Path. A Learning Path is a sequence of learning activities from day one to proficiency. Both of these terms are described in detail with example after example in other chapters in this book. With those definitions out of the way.

Let's start the journey. In 1995, I was working as an instructional designer for a number of very large companies. When you are working on your own, you are never working on just one thing. I had two unique experiences which started me on the road to discovering the Learning Paths approach to training.

As I describe these experiences as well as others in this book, I will refer to these projects without naming the organization and sometimes the industry. This is to make sure that I don't run afoul of any nondisclosure agreement. In many instances, I will be creating a hybrid of two or more organizations with similar issues.

Starting Point

The first key incident involved a large, 1,000 agent hospitality call center. The project involved creating and installing a new process for handling incoming calls. New agents were going to be trained first, and then existing agents were going to be retrained. What was so unique was that this client not only allowed experimentation but encouraged it.

There were four groups of new employees. Two groups would go through the new training, and two groups would go through the existing training. It's very unusual to be given a control group like this. Since calls centers measure almost everything, this made it easier to see the differences and to measure the results.

After the initial weeks of classroom training for the groups on the new process, I was allowed to spend a couple of weeks listening to their calls and making adjustments in the training and in the new sales process. As the agents put their formal training into action, they began to make a series of interesting discoveries.

One of the discoveries they made was that the concept of open and closed questions didn't really work. They did find that certain questions encouraged the customer to talk while others didn't. It wasn't how you asked the question but rather what the question was about that made a difference.

The number one question that got the customer talking was a nice closed question, "Will this be your first time at our resort?" If it was their first time, they couldn't wait to talk about what they wanted to see and do. If they were repeat customers, they talked endlessly about past experiences and how they wanted to replicate them.

As a result, the training was changed from learning open and closed questions to learning the right, battle-tested questions to ask. After two weeks of experimenting, there were more than a dozen changes made to the formal training. It quickly became evident which parts of the training didn't stick and needed to be changed or retrained.

The results were dramatic. There were measurable differences in sales volume and average sale. In addition, there was a reduction in the number of calls that had to be escalated to a supervisor. When these gains were multiplied over the entire call center, the financial gain was truly significant.

I learned three key results of this experience that went into Learning Paths. First, using hard measures to guide and evaluate training makes the training better. Second, testing out training on the job, with real customers yields a range of new best practice ideas. Third, the best way "make trying stick" is to emphasize on-the-job with coaching and feedback to support the formal classroom training.

The second major project involved working with a few thousand travel agents. Before I got there, all the training was done in workshops. They did use audio and video as well, but this was long before e-learning. After conducting a massive amount of upfront research, including mystery shoppers, I was given a free hand to develop a solution. Yes, I could do whatever I wanted.

While I did want to teach an overall sales process, the guiding principle of the new training was to make sure agents used the training, and it improved their overall effectiveness. I decided that the best approach would be to teach one small skill at a time and then move on to the next. The program lasted about 20 weeks with a new topic each week followed by an entire week of practice.

I remember one of the weeks was about listening. Agents were given a self-assessment job aide. For an entire week after each call, they recorded who talk the most, the agent or the customer. At the start of the week, the agent got the most talking checkmarks, but by the end of the week, the customer was doing the majority of the talking.

The goal of each week was to focus on small things that have big effects. Asking each customer if they wanted a car with each trip is small but yields significant results. However, it needs to be a habit if it's going to be done on every call.

Just like the first project, I learned about the value of driving performance measures into training. I learned that focusing on small things with big effects yields quick gains and makes the training easier. When it was done, this project looked significantly more like what I do with current Learning Path projects. It involved moving training out of the classroom and into on-the-job coaching.

Story Continues

The story of Learning Paths continues with a series of projects through 2002, when I began writing the first book. I found that the discipline of sitting down and writing everything into a book crystallized 20 years of thoughts and ideas in a way that I could easily communicate them to others.

Writing has been a part of every job I've had since college. I'm sure it would surprise all my high school teachers that I would have become a published author. My English teachers in both high school and college hated the way I wrote. It wasn't about what I was saying. Instead, it was about their concept of expository writing. They wanted a textbook approach with third person present tense writing. I'm glad I ignored them.

The change came when I started writing history papers in college. Freed from my English teachers, I used my own style. I wrote as if I was talking to someone across the table. Then I would capture what I said to that person.

While I learned to type badly in school, I could basically write or type as fast as I could think. This is similar to the newspaper reporters banging out their stories in the old movies. As a result, teachers found that my writing was not only easy to read but in some cases very entertaining. I remember a comment on a history thesis. The instructor said that I'm going to give you an A, not because of the quality of your research but the fact that I enjoyed reading the paper so much.

Finally, I honed this skill on my first job after college. I worked in an advertising department where I sat behind a typewriter for eight hours a day and wrote ad copy. Spending eight hours a day for two years writing is a good way to write and to write fast.

On the Map

In 2004, the *Learning Paths* book was published. It had the effect of transforming my career from an instructional designer to a training consultant, focusing on building and implementing Learning Paths. I was overwhelmed by the response including all the people who started to follow my writing including several hundred blog posts.

As a result, I was able to put into words what people know intuitively about how people learn. They knew it, but for some reason didn't put into practice very often. There is a great deal of agreement that learning is a process. It's not a one-time event. However, I seldom saw trainers treating learning the same way they treat other processes. Ironically, I never saw quality professionals apply their principles to their own training.

When you look at a process, you try to take out time, waste, and variability. However, it's rare to see anyone take this approach. I've said over the years that there is an array of quality improvement ideas in Learning Paths. I use terms such as Phillip Crosby's "Do It Right the First Time" and Toyota's concept of "Just-in-Time." Those who follow Six Sigma or Kaizen quickly see similarities with Learning Paths.

Since 2004, I've been planning on writing a sequel to the first Learning Paths book. As you can see, it didn't happen overnight. What I wanted to do in this book was to share what I've learned since 2004. Here are some of my big Aha! Moments.

First, I've presented and explained the concepts and principles of Learning Paths several thousand times. I've gotten better and clearer at it. I found that people want more stories and examples as part of the explanation. It's just like Yiddish. In the book *Joys of Yiddish*, Leo Rosten explains that there is a richness to the Yiddish Language. Each word is best understood by a story rather than a straight definition. I remember he explains the difference between the words schlemiel and schlimazel. The schlemiel is the one who always spills the soup, and the schlimazel is the one he always spills it on.

Second, most of the original work was done with large companies that had volumes and volumes of training. Often projects involved reworking existing training including transforming one type of training into another or creating a more blended approach. In the last ten years, I started to work with companies both big and small that had almost no training. In these organizations, most of the training occurred on the job either by trial and error or through working with a co-worker.

Working on all of this informal training was very insightful. Most of it has never been written down. Procedure manuals and work instructions exist, but there are very loose. It's very rare that all stakeholders agree on proficiency or time to proficiency.

Third, I started to work in new industries and with a broader range of jobs. Here are just some of the jobs: insurance sales, forklift operators, clinical nurses, latex operators, truck mechanics, health-care aides, newspaper reporters, hydraulic pump assemblers, newspaper editors, pharmacy techs, front desk agents, housekeeping supervisors, financial planners, mail order pharmacy, railroad conductors, wound care doctors, portable restroom cleaners, credit card debt collectors, and a wide range of salespeople and customer service reps. They are all very different. Each industry claims that they are unique and different. However, there are great similarities in how people learn. The content might be different, but people learn in the same way no matter what the industry is.

Working across industries, I find that great ideas from one industry seem to apply to others quickly. For example, I found that in many different manufacturing jobs, there often isn't enough real-time practice to get good as some of the key elements of the job. Setting up offline practice areas works well whether you're in construction products or food products.

Finally, the internet and social media has become a way of life. Training delivery has moved from paper to the internet, to social media, and to mobile devices. The change in format brings new capability which expands all of the different ways to present, track, and use Learning Paths. Technology has made Learning Paths more robust and easier to use.

One of the most challenging technology issues is to find a learning management system (LMS) or another training manager that is truly calendar based. It's easy to track training but hard to set out a timeline to follow. This timeline is essential for a Learning Path.

As you read this book, you may find some of the ideas very familiar. You may already be using many of them. However, you should find new ideas and stories that you can put into practice. Also, it can help you talk about Learning Paths with others to build support for your initiatives. So I hope you enjoy it.

CHAPTER 2:

The Business Case

I had an opportunity to travel with a small group of senior executives from one of the world's largest travel companies. The occasion was the annual meeting of all the franchisees for a week in the Bahamas.

As we all settled into the rooms, one of the franchise owners called down to the front desk to find out where her luggage was. While she was on hold, she looked out the window and saw her bags running down the beach never to be seen again. At the same time, another attendee opened her bags to find all her jewelry was gone.

The service didn't get any better. At the end of the trip, which took 24 hours to return back to Minneapolis, we missed the connection in Newark and had to go to customer service to reclaim our bags. The agent claimed that our bags weren't there because they were on the flight to Minneapolis. We couldn't understand how our bags made the connection, while we missed it by an hour.

At the customer service counter, the agent became annoyed and began arguing with the top executive of the travel company. Of course, this executive was in charge of all the negotiation with that airline. The conversation ended with the agent saying, "You're an adult, you should know better."

The point of this story is that each interaction with employees who aren't fully trained to deal with these situations could have a substantial financial effect. What do you think resulted in the next negotiations with that airline?

In addition, after the story about the stolen luggage and jewelry rippled through a thousand travel agencies, how do you think that impacted bookings at that resort?

Everyone has similar stories. Employees who aren't fully proficient are expensive. Look at the example of human resources recruiters. In an interview with new candidates, there are some questions they can ask and others they can't. What's the liability of letting a recruiter interview who either wasn't trained on asking interview questions or who passed the test with an 80% score? Every interview becomes a potential lawsuit.

With this in mind, consider that every minute employees are anything less than 100% proficient has a direct, dramatic, and financial impact on an organization. Anything that can shrink time to proficiency is worth considering. Plain and simple, that's the business case for Learning Paths.

Jim Williams, who was the coauthor on the first Learning Paths book, told me that in order to be successful in the training business, you have to learn the language of business, and that language is money. Simply put, time is money. As learning professionals, we help businesses make more money by reducing time to proficiency, time to get up to speed, and time to readiness for promotion. Therefore, the business case for Learning Paths starts by looking at the dollars. Those who are familiar with Six Sigma are very comfortable starting a project with a business case. A solid business case is the best way to create buy-in and executive support.

What's the Cost?

First, let's compare two employees: one who is 70% proficient and one who is 100% proficient. Depending upon the job here are some of the potential differences:

- Lower sales
- Lower productivity
- More errors and rejects
- Poorer quality
- More accidents
- Reduced customer satisfaction
- Additional Rework
- More supervisor time

These are all measurable effects that can be seen in sales numbers, production reports, or customer surveys. The difference between 100% and 70% proficient remains until the gap is closed. As a result, the longer it takes to close that gap, the more it costs. With more hazardous jobs, such as factories that deal with chemicals or high temperatures, there is a greater risk of something bad or catastrophic occurring when untrained employees make mistakes.

Think about the cost of a less than a proficient employee working on a technical helpline. They won't be able to answer 10% to 20% of the problems so someone else will have to handle them. Also, these reps will be giving out considerable wrong information. Everything they got wrong on their tests is now being transferred to customers. In addition, there are jobs where you can't make a mistake such as giving out medications. These employees need to continue in training until they can perform without mistakes. As you begin to dig into what it costs to have an employee not operating at full speed, it's truly significant.

On the other hand, the idea of looking at time-to-proficiency considers the cost difference over time. What's the difference between a salesperson who hits his or her goals in six months versus nine months? What's the difference between a manager who can take on full responsibilities in three months versus one who takes one year? What's the cost of an employee who never gets fully up to speed?

Determining the financial benefits starts by having a clear and detailed description of proficiency. In this book, there is a discussion of how to develop a robust definition of proficiency that is observable and measurable. A proficiency definition can be developed for new employees on their journey to becoming fully independent or for incumbent employees going from average to top performer.

With a proficiency definition in place, it's relatively easy to determine the time to proficiency. Time to proficiency is the key measure for a Learning Path initiative. Without this definition, you can only guess at how long it takes to become proficient.

My experience with hundreds of jobs tells me that it's reasonable to project a minimum 30 percent reduction in time to proficiency using the Learning Paths approach. As you read the next few chapters, you'll see that this is a realistic, if not a conservative estimate. Then you can estimate the potential savings or increased revenue. Also, employees who get up to speed faster than their peers, tend to continue to improve faster because of the solid foundation provided by their Learning Path.

Let's look at some of the other numbers that Learning Paths tend to move as well. The first is turnover or attrition. Employees who aren't up to speed and proficient in their jobs often leave, or worse quit and stay. In addition, these are the employees who tend to be terminated or fired first. To measure the impact on turnover, compare the results of past groups of trainees or new hires with those who have completed their Learning Paths.

Of course, some employees will never become proficient. Some jobs require employees to do high-skill tasks. For example, some jobs require complex mathematical calculations or demanding quality measurements that require a certain aptitude to learn, or at least learn quickly.

In other cases, the employee might have the aptitude but lack motivation or interest. In sales, it's common that some people won't pick up the phone and make cold calls every day. They simply won't.

A Learning Path similarly addresses both these issues. Practicing these required skills becomes part of the Learning Path from the very start. There is no reason to spend six months training a salesperson who simply won't make cold calls.

If an employee simply can't demonstrate the speed and accuracy to do a job without mistakes, it's nice to know that in the first week. Picking orders in a warehouse is one of these jobs. Orders have to be picked in a specified time frame, and they have to be picked without error.

The cost of a mishire, someone who isn't going to make it in a job, is very expensive. Depending upon the job this can easily be between $20,000 and $200,000. This all adds up quickly. In environments where safety is paramount, one additional accident creates millions in extra risk.

Second, there is the cost of retraining. Beyond the cost of extra training, there is the extra time spent by managers and supervisors coaching and correcting employees. Managers often say they don't have the time to train or coach their staff. However, when they don't, they spend a lot of time chasing problems or trying to fix their employees. In an hourly setting, this retraining time is easy to measure because you can see and track the extra hours spent by managers and supervisors.

A Word on Return on Investment (ROI)

In the training industry, there has been a 40-year discussion and sometimes argument on how to measure the financial impact of training. When I see ROI claims for training, it's often something like a 1000%. With a return like that, I wonder why companies wouldn't invest all their money in training. You just can't get that kind of a risk-free ROI with a piece of equipment.

Since there is a gap between the time training ends and performance goals are met, measuring the effects of training can be difficult. As a result, it's hard to prove a cause and effect relationship. Measuring Learning Paths avoids this because the Learning Path isn't over until the higher level of performance is achieved. In other words, training ends when you get the desired level of performance and not until. Therefore, there is a direct relationship between the training and the results.

To illustrate this point, here are few examples. First, a salesperson goes through a five-day sales workshop. In the next few months, sales go up. The cause could be the sales training. It also could be a result of a boom in the market, a new ad campaign, a new product launch or simply the salesperson makes more calls.

Just measuring the results won't provide the answer. You would have to observe the salesperson on the job to see if what was taught in the classroom was actually put into action. You would also have to adjust for any other business factors.

Second, manufacturing employees go through a full day of safety training. In the next two months, accidents go down. It could be the result of the training. It could be caused by a change in the equipment or process. Employees might also have a short-term heightened awareness that will go away over time.

Anytime there is a gap between the end of training and measurement of results, there are always reasonable questions about the cause and effect relationship. Results can vary even if the training didn't transfer to the job.

Therefore, Learning Paths tend to be significantly easier to measure and track to financial results because it's tied directly to performance and changes in performance. Of course, the main measure is time, which is easy to measure on a calendar. It's an overworked cliché, but time is money.

Building Your Own Business Case

Executives like presentations that are short and to the point. You should be able to make the business case for a Learning Path in one page or less. To prepare a business case, you need to know three things. First, what's proficiency for this job? Second, what is the current time to proficiency? Third, what are the most important financial measures? In later chapters, we will cover how to answer these questions.

Here are a few very quick business cases.

Sales

Currently, our salespeople take 18 months to become fully proficient. By reducing time to proficiency by 30%, salespeople will be hitting their targets almost 5 months earlier including bringing in more new customers and taking better care of our current customers.

Manufacturing

Today, our operators take nine months to become fully proficient in their jobs. A reduction in time to proficiency by 30% means that operators will become fully proficient in six months. This reduces your risk of potential accidents by having operators working safely sooner. It means that operators will be hitting production goals sooner with fewer rejects and less scrap.

Healthcare

Currently, our healthcare aides take nearly 7 months to become fully proficient. A reduction in time to proficiency by 30% will have a direct impact on staffing levels because these aides can operate independently earlier. In addition, we expect an increase in customer satisfaction and a reduction in time spent solving problems.

For any job, a business case can be made that reducing time to proficiency is important and financially significant. Thirty percent is what we see every day working across a wide range of jobs and companies. It's often much more than 30%.

In this chapter, I've made some big money claims. In the rest of the book, you'll see how it's possible to make some big gains quickly and then put a process in place to continue to get better and better.

CHAPTER 3:

The Value of Learning Principles

What do you believe is absolutely true about how people learn? The answer to this question is an example of a learning principle. Some people believe that everyone learns differently. Others believe that we learn by doing. Still, others believe that we only learn when we are ready to learn.

There are literally hundreds of learning principles and theories. What's critical is that what we believe drives how we design, deliver, and implement training. For example, if you believe everyone learns differently, training becomes very individualized and self-paced. Different forms of media are matched to suit different learning styles. If you believe we learn by doing, training will have a great deal of practice, simulations, and on-the-job coaching.

In any case, selecting a set of learning principles shapes how companies and organizations train their workforce and develop their leaders. Making the best choices about learning principles will have a direct impact on the effectiveness and cost of their training. It will also have an impact on how fast employees learn.

I've had the privilege of speaking to hundreds of training professionals at major conferences. I always ask them, "What do you believe is absolutely true about how people learn?" I'm always a little bit surprised at their response. The vast majority stop, look up in the air and then think for a while before answering. It's something they may know internally, but they haven't crystalized their thoughts into clear, repeatable statements.

I try to point out to these learning professionals that being able to articulate their learning principles is the first step in moving an organization in the same direction on training. It positions them as the expert in learning rather than just someone who responds to requests to build a training program.

In an organization where learning principles aren't clear, training is different every time a new program is developed. If the organization uses training vendors and consultants, these vendors end up bringing in their own set of learning principles which may be contradictory. In any case, the value of sound and well-articulated learning principles is to take what works the best and makes it universal. This is critical to reducing variability in training.

Also, having a clear set of learning principles saves a lot of time and money. At the start of building a new program, there doesn't have to be a discussion about the best approach. That's already been decided. It's also been determined how the program will be evaluated and what success looks like.

I've found significant value in having a small number of learning principles that are clear, powerful, and universally accepted. With that said, this is the starting point of the discussion about Learning Paths.

The concept of Learning Paths is rooted in three basic learning principles. They are:

- Learning is a process, not an event
- Knowing and doing are not the same thing
- Training should be by design and not by accident

Most people find these principles very intuitive and in line with their own experience. However, they are not always reflected in how people train others. Let's take a look at these three principles in more detail.

Learning Is a Process Not an Event

Consider, is it possible to learn how to sell in a three-day workshop? Can you learn to play tennis in one lesson? Can you learn how to operate machinery safely after five hours of safety training? You could learn some of the basics or have a general understanding of what to do. However, you're a long way away from getting good at any of these tasks.

What's missing? It might be the hours and hours of practice. It could be coaching from an expert, or it just might mean days of real-life experience. In a sales workshop, you might do a half dozen role plays. This doesn't replace the 50 to 100 calls with real customers that it's going to take to ingrain those skills and concepts. One lesson can't substitute for the thousands and thousands of tennis balls required to get good at tennis. Lectures, classes, e-learning courses and more all have their place, but they are only a part of the story.

A learning process is the sequence of all types of learning activities that lead to the desired level of performance. The learning process is a sequence of formal, informal, experiential, and social learning activities from start to finish.

When you start to think of learning as a process, new opportunities open up. You can begin to treat it like any other process and apply what's known about process improvement. These techniques specifically focus on driving out time, waste, and variability. These are not concepts traditionally associated with training, but they are very powerful and relate directly to the cost and effectiveness of training. Let's briefly look at these three concepts, and later in this book we will talk about them in more depth.

Time

Taking a long time to learn something, doesn't add value. Therefore, working on time to proficiency or time to performance has a direct and significant financial importance. In a manufacturing setting, operating safely is of paramount importance. New employees start a manufacturing job unsafe. After training and work experience they become safe on the shop floor. However, the longer it takes, the more likely there will be accidents, spills, and rework. How and when safety training is done will have an impact on the overall amount of time it takes to become safe.

Waste

The definition of waste is anything that doesn't add value. The most obvious source of waste is anything that is taught that the learner doesn't remember a day or a week later. Waste also includes learning something in the classroom that doesn't transfer to the job. This type of waste is usually a result of two factors. First, overloading the learner with content. Learners can only remember and retain so much information. Second, there is not enough practical application to integrate what's being taught where and how it's being used.

Variability

Quality guru Edwards Deming said that variability is the enemy of quality. With high variability, some training will be very good, some very average, and some very bad. In any case, the results are different for every learner. Because the majority of learning occurs on the job, training can vary by trainer, by shift, by supervisor. It can also vary based on when the learner went through training. Last month or a year ago the training was probably different. It's important to point out that training can be highly variable if the work itself is highly variable. Companies that don't have well mapped out processes will find that their training is very inconsistent.

In any attempt to map out the learning process, it almost certain that there is no single learning process. There may be many instead of a single best practices approach. A key part of process improvement is to standardize the process, and then all future improvements are made to one process and not many. When everyone does that work differently, quality suffers. In turn, if the training isn't the same, the results will be all over the board.

Process Mapping

When learning is defined as a process, it can easily be mapped out. Process mapping involves laying out all of the formal, informal, experiential, and social learning activities in sequence from start to finish. The actual activity of laying out a process map of learning activities with experts and stakeholders begins to build that single best practice learning process.

Once the process is mapped, it often becomes very obvious where the opportunities for improvement lie. It's easy to see that:

- The process is incomplete
- Too many activities happen in the first week or two
- Activities are out of sequence
- Some activities are duplicated or unnecessary

Looking at learning as a process and not an event changes how an organization looks at training. It goes well beyond building workshops and e-learning. It becomes more about performance and using training to shape how work gets done.

Knowing and Doing Are Not the Same

There is an old saying that "knowledge is power." In reality being able to use that knowledge is the real power. Knowing and doing are not only not the same, but they are miles apart. Knowing how to sell and actually making sales is very different. Knowing the answer to questions about a product is one thing, being able to answer those questions with a customer in a positive and timely manner is completely different. Knowing the trends in the marketplaces is vastly different from building and implementing a plan to take advantage of those.

All too often training and education have been focused on knowledge acquisition. It's easy to teach, and it's easy to test. Lectures, classroom, webinars, and e-learning are simple ways to impart knowledge. However, it doesn't mean any of the training will transfer to the job. The real challenge of training is to make that leap out of everyone's head and into action.

When you adopt the principle of knowing is not doing, it changes how you design, deliver, and implement training. First, the training objectives read more like performance statements with actual numbers and measures. Instead of using words such as know, understand, comprehend, and aware, you see words such as operate, sell, produce, plan, and lead. Knowledge objectives can be met in an e-learning course, but performance-based objectives are met through a long process that includes extensive practice, experience, and feedback.

With the Learning Paths Methodology, instead of learning objectives, we use a proficiency definition which describes the required level of performance in terms of how good, how much, how fast, and how safe. In other words, quality, output, speed, and safety.

This principle dramatically changes how learners and training are evaluated. Instead of multiple choice knowledge tests, evaluation is done in two ways. First, performance on-the-job can be directly observed by an expert. "Experts know it when they see it." Think about evaluating agents in a call center. You can observe and hear how they interact with customers and how they handle tough questions. You see how they navigate from screen to screen and how quickly they find answers.

I think one of the more interesting examples is to watch someone pick an order using a forklift. Someone who isn't proficient will waste time trying to find the order and maybe hit a few boxes and pallets along the way. The proficient forklift operator will make a beeline to the order and quickly and safely pull it. Even if the difference between these two workers is only a few minutes, over the course of a week or month that's a lot of time.

Second, training designed to change performance can be measured by the numbers. In a call center, it might be the number of calls handled, number of escalations to a supervisor, talk time, and even customer satisfaction rating. For a salesperson, it might be number of calls made, sales volume, profitability on sales, number of new customers, and maybe the number of referrals. Therefore, along with observations, looking at the numbers makes a robust way of evaluation.

Getting 100% on a multiple-choice test doesn't mean the learner can put any of that knowledge into action. When the focus is on doing rather than just knowing, the knowledge builds as it's needed during practical application.

Training Should Be by Design and Not by Accident

Most learning happens on-the-job and informally after the formal training ends. Almost every study I've ever seen says that informal learning is between 70% and 90% of all learning. Unfortunately, most of this learning is haphazard, highly unstructured, and filled with trial and error. It's different for everyone, so it creates a high degree of variability. As a result, some learners will take a very long time to become proficient, and some will never get there.

Most informal training leaves the realm of the training department and happens outside of their reach or control. It's managers and supervisors who need to do this training and see that it gets done. However, managers often say they don't have time to coach their people. They also aren't prepared to do it although they do have the time. As a result, this informal training or coaching is done by another employee who is even less prepared.

When training happens by design rather than by accident, there is a structure and process to makes sure learning is complete, effective, and timely. For example, companies frequently use joint calls or ride alongs to train salespeople. New salespeople are simply sent out with a more experienced salesperson or sales manager. However, there is usually no process or structure to these joint calls, so it's uncertain what will happen. As a result, they often fall into the category of waste.

In call centers, many new employees learn from the person sitting next to them. That's great if these people are well trained and good at their jobs. However, their neighbor doesn't know everything and may have developed undesirable shortcuts and workarounds to get through the day.

In a manufacturing setting, it's critical to know what to do when the process starts to go off-track. Instead of teaching the new operator how to handle these situations, the person doing the coaching takes over and does it instead.

With this principle, there is a disciplined plan for practice, coaching, and feedback after formal training ends. There are detailed instructions for coaches and mentors with a range of job aides to help them do their jobs. While this can take more time to develop and implement, once in place, it saves time because there isn't as great a need to do constant retraining.

A typical Learning Path for a job might have 50 to 100 learning activities. The vast majority are designed to structure on the job training and learning experiences. Later in this book, there is a detailed discussion on how to build informal and on-the-job activities in a way that makes them more intentional and structured.

In this chapter, we've examined the role that learning principles play in shaping how we design, deliver, and implement training. What we believe does make a big difference. With the Learning Path Methodology, I've boiled down these principles to three easy-to-remember but powerful statements. In the end, I believe that learning is a process and is most beneficial when it builds and improves how we perform. Finally, as learning leaders, it should be our job to make this happen by intention rather than hoping it gets done.

CHAPTER 4:

Starting on the Same Page

The three Learning Path Principles are the foundation for the three Learning Path Concepts. This chapter sets out the definitions for the three concepts—Proficiency, Learning Path, and Time to Proficiency. While these terms are defined differently by different people, I've been trying to create a common language and standard for these terms. It's easier if we are all on the same page.

Proficiency

Proficiency is defined as a "required" level of performance. As shown in the chart below, proficiency is defined in terms of output, quality, speed, and safety. In other words, how much, how good, how fast, and how safe.

Proficiency is the end result of a Learning Path. The idea of a "required" level of performance means that an employee must meet or exceed to successfully complete a Learning Path. New and experienced employees have a different level of performance. Proficiency levels can be in stages rather than having everyone shoot for the top all at once.

In some environments, the concept of a required level of performance is very clear. In sales, there is a break-even point where the new employee generates a high enough level of revenue to cover their base salary. A new salesperson must achieve this level of sales as quickly as possible.

In a manufacturing plant, there are minimum standards for accuracy, production, and safety. Minimum doesn't mean low; it means this is an absolute measure. 85% isn't acceptable. There can also be a required level set for a top performer. This is often the same measures with a much higher standard.

Let's look at each of the components of proficiency in more detail.

Output

The output is a measure of what or how much an employee produces. For most jobs, the output is very tangible and concrete. Output is usually a key business measure as well.

Output for a salesperson is clear. It's revenue, new customers, proposals, etc. Factory workers produce package and ship parts. Output is trickier for management and position of leadership. However, leaders produce outcomes such as visions, functioning teams, and motivated workforces. It's a very interesting discussion to look at the difference between the traits of a leader and what a leader actually produces. Toward the end of the book, there is a chapter about working on leadership development.

Quality

Quality is a further description of the output. Quantity and quality go hand in hand. Quality indicators might include: reject rate, profitability, spills, or customer satisfaction rating. There is often a quality standard for products and services such as standard operating procedures (SOPs) or standard work documents. When producing work, the SOP or standard work becomes one of the quality indicators. Mixing 15 vats of resin per day according to SOP 1592 adds needed detail to the quality of how this work should be done.

Speed

The concept of speed is an interesting one. Speed, as it relates to proficiency, doesn't mean rushing or carelessness. Speed means accomplishing tasks in an acceptable time frame. When employees become more proficient, speed naturally increases. As tasks become second nature, there is a fluidity and confidence in their motion. Watch anyone who is outstanding at something, and they will be considerably faster than a beginner.

Interestingly enough, the fastest way to increase speed is to do things right the first time. If rushing and carelessness lead to rejects and rework, the employee is slower. Measure twice and cut once is faster than measuring once and then having to start all over again when the measurement was wrong.

Here's another example of how speed relates to proficiency. One of the most common performance measures in a call center is talk time. Talk time is the average time it takes to handle a call. This can be controversial because some calls do take longer than others. The time of any single call can vary greatly, but over a 100 or even a 1000 calls, there will be a consistent average. The goal is not to take calls as fast possible but instead to meet a reasonable average for successful agents.

During training, some agents are slower than others because they haven't mastered how to use the phone, their computer and talk to the customer at the same time. Others are slower because their keyboard skills need work, and still others are slow because they aren't proficient in the flow of the conversation. Slowness can be a key indicator that more training, practice, and feedback are needed.

On the other side, some agents are faster than others. It's possible that they are just that much better at multi-tasking and comfortable in the call center setting. However, it may be a warning sign that they are skipping something or they are not fully following procedures. They may be so focused on speed that they've gotten careless. Instead of ignoring the speedsters, it's important to see if they are meeting the proficiency standards.

Safety

Safety is a critical measure used in manufacturing, healthcare, food services and other hazardous jobs. In fact, safety becomes the most important measure. The minimum level of safety might be operating 100% safely at all times.

However, a new employee may not be involved in the same activities of a top performer. For example, a new maintenance employee may not fix electrical problems while a top performer might. So the definition of proficiency for a new employee will be different from a more experienced employee.

Proficiency Definitions

Most jobs are multifaceted with a wide range of tasks and responsibilities. To define the whole job, a proficiency definition consists of a number of proficiency statements. A good proficiency definition consists of about 20 to 60 statements depending upon the complexity of the job. There will be more statements for a software engineer than a job doing packaging on an assembly line.

In this book, there will be more about how to write these statements. In general, proficiency statements describe how the job is done and the required output or results. Again, they focus on output, quality, speed, and safety or how good, how much, how fast, and how safe. Here are just a few examples of what proficiency statements are like. Notice all the output numbers and quality measures.

Sales

Builds and maintains a pipeline in the customer relationship management (CRM) of at least 150 qualified prospects with the potential of $7,500 revenue in each

Manufacturing

Charges ammonia in tanks and jugs within +/-2% following SOP 1820

Call Center

Resolves 95% of all customer technical issues using the problem-solving process check sheet without escalation and within 5 minutes

Health Care

Follows the daily care plan to attend to all of the client's hygiene requirements according to company policy and state regulations achieving a minimum of 4.5 out of 5 in client satisfaction ratings

Mechanics

Changes oil within 15 minutes on both trucks and cars without spills while following all OSHA guidelines

Proficiency vs. Competency vs. Learning Objectives

A discussion of proficiency isn't complete without a comparison with the two other common training terms, competency and learning objectives. Competency models break down a job or task in terms of knowledge, skills, and attitudes or sometimes attributes. Everybody does this slightly differently, but for the most part, this is a common definition. Competency Models are used for training, hiring, and performance appraisals.

As you can see, knowledge, skills, and attitudes are very different from output, quality, speed, and safety. Competencies are more about what you know and have the ability to do rather than what you produce. Here are some examples that show the difference between a proficiency statement and a competency statement.

Competency

- Understands the issues and trends of our industry

Proficiency

- Creates a competitive advantage by building and implementing a marketing plan that responds to the issues and trends of our industry

Competency

- Understands the issues and trends of our industry

Proficiency

- Creates a competitive advantage by building and implementing a marketing plan that responds to the issues and trends of our industry

Competency

- Can troubleshoot production problems by applying effective problem-solving techniques

Proficiency

- Creates a competitive advantage by building and implementing a marketing plan that responds to the issues and trends of our industry
- Resolves production problems following appropriate SOPs without shutting down the line

Competency

- Knows how to resolve team conflicts by accounting for differences in communication styles

Proficiency

- Maintains team's schedule and plan by identifying and resolving team conflicts from differences in communication styles

Competency models seldom include any numbers. That's because they are not specifically tied to the outputs or results of a job. Some competency modules will have behavioral statements which further define how a skill is done.

With competencies, training gets done by aligning each competency with a training program or part of a training program. For example, team building or communication skills are identified as a competency, and as a result, there is a team building and communications course.

Proficiency statements don't work that way. Training is designed to achieve all of the proficiency statements. One statement may be part of several learning activities while another learning activity might cover several learning activities. As we talk about building Learning Paths, this difference comes to light.

As you look at a proficiency statement, you won't see any statements that start with the words, know, understand, or aware. Remember that knowing and doing aren't the same thing. The proficiency statements will talk about the results when that knowledge, understanding, or awareness is put into action. It's not *knowing what's new or trending in the market* that's important; rather it's what you do with it.

Finally, when you list out all the required skills and knowledge, you miss how these skills and knowledge work together or are done at the same time. As a colleague reminded me, it's not walk, chew gum, it's walk and chew gum.

A better example might be that you can know all the features and benefits of a product. However, the proficiency is to describe these features and benefits to a customer in a way that gets them to respond positively and answers their questions.

To illustrate this, I had an interesting discussion about this with a friend from Century College in Minnesota. Century is well known for being a leader in competency-based education. He explained that teaching competencies only goes so far when preparing students for real work situations. Being a master at doing a brake job isn't the full job. It's learning how to work with other employees in the garage and managing this task with five other staff members while explaining to the customer why this is going to cost $500.

While learning how to do a brake job might take a week or two, becoming proficient at doing in a real-life situation might take six months to a year. This is an approach that not only identifies all the pieces in the puzzle but how they fit together.

Learning objectives, on the other hand, are something completely different. Learning objectives try to define what the student or learner will get out of a piece of training or learning activity. For example, they complete the statement, "As a result of this training, the student will be able to...."

Learning Objectives are much smaller and confined to a specific learning activity. Taking the proficiency statement "Sells $15,000 per month at a 15% profitability," a series of learning objectives would define what the salesperson would need to learn to reach this proficiency. So learning objectives are valuable design tools, but they are not the same as proficiencies. Learning objectives are used in the same way with competencies.

I was like a lot of people who studied education in college. We read the book *Bloom's Taxonomy*. I still have an old and dusty copy. It did a great job of explaining how to write learning objectives and it presented a great list of words that could be used to write any learning objective. Know, understand, aware, explain, demonstrate, list, and analyze all made it on the list. It's a very useful tool. However, it was geared to school-based education. Came in handy for a high school history teacher. What I've found more useful is to create a list of action verbs that include business terms and what people do on-the-job. These words include: sell, inspect, load, package, plan, promote, and process. When I do Learning Paths workshops, I have participants review this list, and then add all of the words that relate to their company and their jobs.

I tried to apply Bloom's Taxonomy when I did student teaching at an inner-city high school in Minneapolis. I worked with two history teachers who were known as the Warner Brothers. They got that name because they showed endless filmstrips and movies, almost every class. When I got my evaluation, the comment was, "Did well but could have shown more movies."

Learning Path

Now that we have a good definition of proficiency let's define Learning Path. While there are many different ways people define Learning Path and others use it as an interchangeable term with Training Plan, I've been trying to get others to adopt this definition as an industry standard. It just helps us all speak the same language.

The way I define a Learning Path is that it's the sequence of Learning Activities from the start of training until the learner become proficient. When defining a Learning Path, it's important to define a learning activity. I define it broadly as anything the learner goes through that leads to proficiency. There are books that describe hundreds of different learning activities. All of these could find their way onto a Learning Path. It's both the formal and informal training.

For the sake of defining terms, generally, formal training includes classroom, webinars, videos, e-learning, and anything that has a formal structure. Informal training refers to any learning that is live and on-the-job. It's practice, coaching, experience, and interacting with others. Informal training even happens when you're just wandering around. A Learning Path needs to cover it all.

One of the major challenges in mapping a learning path is the large percentage of informal learning. All of the studies I've ever seen say that between 70% and 90% of all learning occurs informally. Most informal training is not documented and different for every learner. The amount of variability in most learning paths is significant. The immediate way to improve a Learning Path is to take all the variations of Learning Paths and create one best practice Learning Path.

The second challenge of using the Learning Path approach is that it's a sequence of learning activities rather than a pick and choose model. The correct sequence is designed by experts who know what needs to be on the path and the fastest way to complete it. Remember that if Learning is a process, it can be mapped out as one path.

Today's technology makes it possible for learners to learn what they want and when they want to learn it. But just because it's easy and comfortable doesn't mean it's the fastest or most effective. Here's an example.

In the movie *Karate Kid*, a young boy learns karate in a few short weeks under the guidance of Mr. Miagi who has been studying Karate for all his life. He puts Daniel, the kid, on a Learning Path where he starts by washing cars, painting a fence, and sanding floors. Daniel objects but he quickly learns that each of these tasks built the motor memory of key karate moves. Now, if you let a new student pick and choose how to learn karate, I can't imagine any of them choosing "wash the car" or "paint the fence."

When doing training needs analysis, it's common to ask experts what needs to be learned. Perhaps the better and more powerful question is to ask, "How did you actually learn to be good at this?" The experts are the ones who know about all the informal learning on-the-job and what worked and what didn't. They will also know what they tried that didn't work. An effective way to speed up learning is to limit all the wrong twist and turns along the way.

Finally, the expression, "it depends" stands in the way of working on learning as a process. Some people can think of hundreds and even thousands of potential variations and differences that could make it impossible to map out the learning process. Here's what they say:

- Everyone's different there is no common theme
- We can't rely on scheduling training on any given day
- Things happen! You won't get three activities in before you have to make a change
- No one has time for this

I respond to this in a couple of different ways. First, a Learning Path is a plan like any other plan. You map out what you think will work the best and them make adjustments as you go. You can't map out 50 different Learning Paths; you need to work with one. It's a matter of using your best judgment and then trying it out before giving up.

Second, certain ways of learning are universal. No one masters the piano without hours and hours of practice. No one learns to swim until he or she gets into the pool. Nobody learns to sell until they've been in front of customers.

Apprenticeships

Apprenticeships have been a powerful way to learn for centuries. In many respects, Learning Paths mirror what apprenticeship programs do. Transferring knowledge and skills from experts is a key part of becoming the master.

However, setting up apprenticeships isn't feasible when a 1000 students are waiting to learn. There simply aren't enough master to go around. Apprenticeship programs are often time-limited. For example, an apprenticeship might be 2000 hours. In the end, these time constraints are arbitrary or wild guesses. It's amazing that so many apprenticeship programs last the same amount of time or are completed in nice round numbers.

A Learning Path is going to look at how to replicate the good parts of apprenticeship in a way that can be replicated with a large number of students without the high variability of individual masters.

Customizing the Path

It's true that no two learners start a Learning Path with the same level of experience or ability. Therefore, the goal is to create a Learning Path that is flexible enough to accommodate all learners. The answer is to create a complete path for the least experienced employee from start to finish. No one is going to need more training than the beginners Learning Path.

Now to customize the path for more experienced employees simply cross off or modify the unnecessary learning activities. For example, if an experienced travel agent has already completed the Mexico specialist program, they don't have to repeat it.

While this approach accounts for all different types of learners, it's making sure that nothing is missed. It's also easy to underestimate what experienced workers need. I worked with a company that hired CPAs to close out their books every year. They thought these employees didn't need very much training because after all, they were CPAs. While working on a Learning Path, it became clear that there was so much nuance and complexity in how the books were done, that the current staff was taking almost two years to become proficient. They didn't have to go through all the basics, but there was so much more company information that still needed to be learned.

Time to Proficiency

Time to proficiency is the overall goal and measurement of a Learning Path initiative. Time to proficiency is the total time it takes to go from a starting point to proficiency. It's not the time spent in the classroom but rather all of the formal and informal learning.

Measuring time to proficiency starts by having a robust proficiency definition that is shared and agreed upon by everyone. Then time to proficiency can be determined by historical measurements and surveying experts in the job. When looking at sales or production data, it's easy to see when the last group of new employees started to hit their numbers. Unfortunately for some jobs and in some organizations, there isn't very much performance data. In those cases, they have to rely on expert observation. However, the Learning Path initiative becomes their first start on getting and using performance data.

On the first pass, current time to proficiency becomes a baseline measure for comparing progress after the Learning Path is implemented. It's not critical to determine proficiency to the hour, day, or sometimes week. Through the Learning Path methodology, this number is going to move dramatically, and the gains will be significant.

Just a word of caution. When there are only a few employees in a position, time to proficiency will vary greatly. It's hard to get a meaningful estimate of time to proficiency for two people. However, if there are 20 or 200, the number is much more consistent.

At the start of a Learning Path project, I always ask the experts and the other stakeholders how long it takes for a new employee to become proficient in a specific job. The more people asked, the wider the range of answers. Some say it's two or three weeks, while others say it's 18 to 24 months. Then after building a proficiency definition, I ask the question again but say, how long does it take for a new employee to look like this? The answer is usually "Oh! That's a different story that's more like 18 months."

In the past, a first time Learning Path initiative reduced time to proficiency by at least 30%, which is a big deal. However, when you look at the overall timeline not just the time in training, there is enough waste and variability in the learning process, that 30% is actually an easy number to hit.

In working with a very large bank, just rearranging their Learning Path to focus on "Doing things right the first time," cut time to proficiency by two thirds. There is usually enough waste and variability in any path to rapidly reduce time to proficiency.

Another key area in cutting time to proficiency comes from structuring all of the informal learning. This includes setting up time for practice and providing coaches with tools to facilitate that practice. Throughout this book, there will be example after example of different ways to cut time to proficiency.

When working on time to proficiency, management quickly realizes that a percentage of the existing workforce isn't fully proficient. To retrain these employees doesn't require a new Learning Path. Instead, the Learning Path can be customized for each employee based on their level of experience and what they need.

I remember working on building a proficiency definition for senior software engineers. In those days, we'd create these on flip charts or whiteboards. In their conference room, they had whiteboards on all four walls. Every inch of the whiteboards was covered with proficiency statements. Two engineers, who had been there for 5 years, looked at one of the panels and commented that they were never trained on how to do those items. The boss was surprised because those proficiencies were critical to this job.

I just want to reinforce that time to proficiency is different from time to the end of training. This is important in building and presenting your business case. Training might end in two weeks, but proficiency might not be achieved for nine months. The 30% reduction in time to proficiency we typically get is based on the nine months, not the two weeks.

This covers the three concepts of Learning Paths that go hand in hand with the three principles. Just having a common language is a big step on the way to improvement. If learning is a process, not an event, then a Learning Path becomes that process which opens up many ways to improve training. It's a big step to making training happen by design rather than by accident, by structuring all of the informal training. Finally, since knowing and doing aren't the same, a proficiency definition is a very robust way of making sure we are focusing on the doing side.

Learning Paths Methodology

The rest of this book shows how to reduce time to proficiency by following the Learning Paths Methodology. Here is a high-level look at the overall approach.

1. **Select a Function**

    The first step is to select a function, task, or job. Select some that will have an immediate and significant impact if time to proficiency is slashed.

2. **Form a Learning Path Team**

    Second, assemble a team of stakeholders to work on this initiative. The next chapter goes into great detail on who should be on this team.

3. **Define Proficiency**

    Now the process begins. This process mirrors the way continuous improvement is done and can be repeated to continue to shrink time to proficiency. The Learning Path team starts by defining proficiency including measuring current time to proficiency.

4. **Map the Current Path**

    With a robust proficiency definition in place, the team then goes on to map out the current Learning Path. In other words, what's the path to proficiency today?

5. **Identify Opportunities for Improvement**

Then through applying process improvement, accelerated learning, and change management techniques, the team identifies a large number of opportunities to speed up the Learning Path.

6. **Upgrade the Learning Path**

The next step is to create an upgraded Learning Path using the improvement ideas generated by the team. The upgraded path will be at least 30% faster.

7. **Create Learning Activities**

For every activity on a Learning Path, the team creates a detailed activity description. In many cases, these activity descriptions become the recipe book for all of the informal learning.

8. **Implement and Maintain**

The final step is to implement and maintain the new Learning Path. This includes measuring results and reporting back on the business case.

Again, this is only a high-level view. However, it provides context for the rest of this discussion in this book. It puts everything into perspective. If you have a lot of questions at this point, that's great because answering those questions is a goal of this book.

CHAPTER 5:

Relying on the Experts

I have a quick little story about becoming an expert I'd like to share before talking about how to get the most out of using experts. I feel that credibility is the key attribute of an expert. This means that others believe you know what you're doing and will follow you.

Over the years, I've found that there are three levels of credibility. When you are young and just starting out in training, others will tell you what to do. They'll say, "Give me a team building course or some sales training." If you object, they will simply say, "I don't care just do it."

As you get older and wiser, all of a sudden you hear, "You're the expert, you tell me." It's surprising the first time you hear. I sometimes hear this as "You wrote the book on that, you tell me."

I discovered the final level when I was giving a speech to the Chinese Society of Training and Development. I spoke to an audience of over 1,100. Several people after the end of the speech told me they liked some of my jokes. I couldn't remember telling any jokes. I think one of the people who were translating added in a few choice comments, but I had no way of knowing.

At that conference, my partner had a very large booth for Learning Paths. He had arranged for about 19 college-age interns to work the booth. A group of three of the interns came up to me at the end of the speech and said, "Mr. Steve, we want to be like you when we grow up." That either means I was starting to get old or I had reached the final rung on the credibility ladder.

Finding Experts

Who are the experts? Anyone who does or supervises the job can be an expert. It can be others who have a stake in the process. Working on a Learning Path requires a team of these experts.

Quality circles were very big when I started in the training business. In those days, Edwards Deming, Joseph Juran, and Phillip Crosby were the gurus of the quality movement. Although Deming, Juran, and Crosby sound like a singing group, they revolutionized the way we look at quality. I met Deming once when he was almost ninety.

Quality Circles brought a unique way for those involved at all levels of an organization to work together on a common goal of improving quality. Over time, a similar approach was used for both Six Sigma and Kaizen. So working on Learning Paths makes a great deal of sense because there are significant benefits of having a team work on improving the way people learn.

The difference between how I work with these teams now versus 15 years ago is radically different. I learned more about what these teams did well, what they didn't do as well, and what was a waste of their time. Today, I'm more flexible. However, there are some universal truths about these teams.

Forming Teams

Let's look at who should be on these teams and how many people should work on a Learning Path team. First, I try to get as many people on these teams as I can. In many respects, Learning Path teams are used to build support and consensus while avoiding being looked at as the flavor of the month. Ask, whose input will be valuable and who needs to support this effort?

I've worked with teams as small as three and as large as twenty. The ideal number is somewhere in between depending on how well the project leader can facilitate a larger group. With a large team, most of the review process happens with the team. With small teams, the work product of the team ends up being circulated to a larger number of key stakeholders for review, input, and in some cases approval.

Project Champion

Let's start with the most important person on a Learning Path team, the project champion. Every Six Sigma project has a project champion, but this is slightly different. A project champion is almost always someone at a Vice President or high level. The qualities of a project champion are some who has:

- Fully embraced the Learning Paths approach
- A financial stake in the outcome
- Operations or sales areas responsibilities. Sometimes, the project champion comes from human resources, quality, or even safety
- Authority to act quickly and get results without layers of approval

Here is an example of the power of a good project champion. I was leading a team for a major healthcare company. The team came up with several procedural changes to make the training more effective. However, the team members didn't have the authority to make those changes. Fortunately, the senior vice president of operation was the project champion and was sitting in on all meetings. Once he heard the justification for the changes, instead of taking weeks or month, he just said, "Okay, the decision is made, the procedures are now changed." That's what a good project champion can do.

Once the project champion is in place, there are many good choices for team members. Often these people will be nominated by the project champion. When you have a good project champion, you get an assortment willing volunteers. I've always related it to what my father did when we were growing up. He seldom told us what to do, but would say, "You know, you really should." So when the president invites a plant manager to get involved by saying, "you don't have to, but you really should," the plant manager shows up.

Project Leader

The second person to consider is the project leader. Qualities of a good project leader are some who can:

- Lead or facilitate all of the team interactions including creating team consensus
- Manage this initiative as a well-run project.

A project leader is usually a senior HR leader, training manager, or consultant. This has to be someone that the team will respect.

Stakeholders

The next group of team members are those who know how the job is done and those who know how the job is managed. It could be plant managers, production managers, shift managers, and operators. It could be salespeople and sales managers.

Consider those who are impacted by this job such as production schedule, shipping, order entry, or customer service. Choose those individuals whom others respect and follow. There is an opportunity to involve others as subject matter experts and reviewers but not part of the team.

Other Departments

Some of the departments that might contribute or benefit from being on a Learning Path team include human resources, quality, finance, and safety. Every job tends to touch these areas. Human resources can play a big role on a Learning Path team. HR is the keeper of many of the documents that provide useful information such as job descriptions, performance appraisal forms, and competency studies. HR can also speak to any pre-hire testing both current and historical.

In return, HR gets a lot out of being on a Learning Path team. One HR director remarked after sitting on a Learning Path team is that she had been hiring for this position for ten years but that this was the first time she understood what these front-line workers did every day. The amount of detail was something that could only come from those working in the plant every day. As a result, she was able to reassess the hiring profile and adjust some of the pre-hire testing.

HR is often the link to some of the online systems that can be used to deliver a Learning Path such as a Human Resource Information System (HRIS) and an LMS. Just a side note. One of the big problems with this software or in fact any software is that it doesn't come with any content. Some may provide access to large numbers of generic courses, but they don't have the detailed training for each job. A Learning Path initiative is going to provide this content for both the formal and informal training. Learning Paths enable better performance tracking and reporting.

A well-implemented Learning Path will provide key information about an employee's performance throughout the training period. This includes any testing or observation of on-the-job performance. HR will find this valuable for documenting any termination or promotion to the next level.

The quality department can add value as well. I was working with a team in a small manufacturing company. The training leader said to me that all this measurement was extremely valuable but that he didn't know how to do it. I turned to the quality manager and asked, "Do you know how to measure this?" He said, "Sure that's easy." The quality staff is usually trained in measurement and statistics and can do all the math. They work with measuring other processes, at least from the math side, isn't difficult for them. They don't have a blank stare in reaction to the words, regression analysis.

What often amazes me about quality departments is that they do a great job with every process in the company, except learning. Their training tends to be a mixture of classroom and e-learning without many activities to transfer learning to the job. In contrast, one of the original projects was to design and implement a Learning Path for quality Black Belts. Black Belts are a Six Sigma designation for those who are training to lead major quality projects. The result of this project was that new Black Belts finished their first project 6 months earlier than their counterparts and then continued to do projects even faster over time.

Finance provides the other side of the measurement. In other words, how to translate results into financial measures that senior executives care about. If you're going to make big claims, it helps to have a business accountant review the numbers. Early on there was more effort focused on proving the financial results of a Learning Path. However, after a while, I kept getting this typical response from the top executive "Don't waste your time, I get it, it's a lot of money." Because Learning Paths will move the numbers, it often is very obvious. When salespeople hit their goals six months earlier, everyone gets it that it's significant.

I sometimes get the question, "Can we put a customer or supplier on the team?" I think both can add a great deal of value. However, it's hard to schedule their time. It's usually better to plan to interview them during the research stage. This avoids any confidentiality issues.

When building a Learning Path, customers and suppliers can be a good source of existing training. This is perfect especially when it's free. They might be a good source of pictures and video.

Team Rules and Norms

With the team selected, the next step is to define the roles and rules for the team. The roles are fairly clear. The project champion is there to make things happen and remove any barriers to the team's success. The project leader's role is to facilitate meetings and to keep this running smoothly. The project champion and the project leader will be managing the scope of the Learning Path project.

Working on a Learning Path will surface other issues in the organization. Those need to be saved for another project and another day. A Learning Path project can take forever if the team is allowed to take side trips or argue about unrelated issues. Try to keep a very tight scope for each Learning Path project.

Team members are there to participate and contribute actively. Make it clear that there are no bystanders on a Learning Path team. No one gets to play the role of passive observer. If anyone is going to be on the team, we are going to put them to work. If someone doesn't have time to be on the team, they should be asked to be a reviewer or be on the interview list. Team meetings are always very interactive and designed to get everyone involved.

Personally, I don't like to run a Learning Path team in secret. If anyone wants to know what's going on, I tell them. However, it's important to set it up properly. Let others know what the Learning Path team is working on to make our training better and that we welcome any ideas that will help. A Learning Path project is not problem-solving but rather process improvement. Even if we are the best in the world, there is always room for improvement. Most people see the value in better, more effective training.

I haven't mentioned the training department yet, but trainers and instructional designers may be more involved than anybody. Trainers often know what's in the current training and how it's delivered. They often know what works and what doesn't. Even if they don't, trainers are going to be involved in implementing the training, so they have to buy into the end product.

I worked in a very large call center that had a new hire class of twenty starting almost every week. I had the trainers meet as a review team, and each one said to me, "You know, this is the first time anyone asked us about what should be in the new hire training." This is a sure recipe for trainers to ignore what's been written and do their own thing in the classroom. As a result, every class was different.

Learning Paths do require writing. This is not something most people do every day, and so it can be challenging. Trainers and especially instructional designers do this type of writing, and many are very, very good at it. The good ones know how to take what an expert says and translate it into simple, everyday language. Writing every day for a few years rapidly sharpens up this skill.

That's the team. A Learning Path team is there to get critical information and generate new ideas as well as build support and consensus. Any new training program is going to create change, so treat it as a change management project.

A final note on keeping a Learning Path team on track. Often, HR and training have learned a wide range of approaches and methodology. They will try to introduce these models as an approach they like better. The only way to respond to this is that these are all great models, but we aren't going to use them today. If we are going to keep on track, we have to stick with the process. The project leader has to be the keeper of the process and not let other models derail the team. It's simply a discussion that isn't necessary. In addition, this is the process that project champion wants to follow.

Eliminating the Blank Page

In working with the Learning Path team, there is one very significant change that I've made over the years. Traditional brainstorming is time-consuming and doesn't yield the critical and new thinking that leads to improvement.

Try this experiment, and you will see what I mean. Bring a group of managers together and ask them to brainstorm a list of the qualities of a great salesperson. After an hour, you will have a list of the obvious. Eighty to ninety percent of this will be a list you could have created in about five minutes on your own. We all know they have to handle objections and close sales.

What works better is to create the list of the obvious and then let the team react to it. Ask the questions:

- What would you add?
- What would you delete?
- What would you modify?
- How is this unique to us?

So instead of asking the question, "What's proficiency for a given job?" I take this approach. I do enough upfront research to create a draft. I tell the team that I've got about 70% to 80% of it right. Then the team works on making it better. The result is that the proficiency definition takes less time to complete and it's at least one generation better. Most people have a terrible time working from a blank flip chart page or sheet of paper. They are so much better at reacting to something already written. Here's an example of how the discussion changes:

Part of a proficiency statement might be to sell at least $7,500 a month. The discussion will be about whether $7500 right or should it be $10,000? Team members will disagree, often vehemently, but this is an important discussion to have. The team spends more time adding measures and quality indicators to make the definition more robust and accountable.

At the end of the process of building a proficiency statement, the team should be able to say, "This is the results we expect." By defining the endpoint, the process to get there can easily be determined.

That's the basics of a Learning Path team. While having a great project leader is a must, I can't overemphasize the importance of a good project champion. When the question comes up about which job or function to start with, I'd always recommend the one that has a committed project champion.

CHAPTER 6:

Do You Know It When You See It?

Today, football, baseball, basketball, and hockey measure almost everything. These sports have become games of statistics and statistical analysis. However, they do one other thing to evaluate the performance of their players. Coaches and managers review hours and hours of film looking at all those actions that can't be easily measured and how players react to a wide range of real-life situations. Proficiency is something that you can measure, but it's also something that can be seen if you know what to look for.

Some things aren't obvious to the casual onlooker or average performer. However, an expert can see all of the details and nuance. If you've ever watched gymnastics or figure skating, the expert commentator sees all sorts of flaws even though the routines look flawless. It's always preferred to have expert observations, but it's possible for others to do observations with performance standards and checklists. A proficiency definition is set up to define and guide measurement and observation.

Let's talk about the three parts of a proficiency definition including how to develop the definition and how to make it useful. The first part of a proficiency definition is the individual proficiency statements. Keep in mind that a proficiency definition consists of a number of individual proficiency statements.

Categories

While it might sound backward, I find that the easiest way to identify proficiency statements is first to identify about five to ten categories. A category is a logical grouping of tasks or performance measures. It's a process of starting by labeling all the file folders before starting to write anything.

There is no set order for these categories. If a different order makes more sense, these categories can be rearranged. These categories can be renamed, combined or tossed out as you go along. They are just a way to get organized and make it possible to work on one thing at a time rather than everything all at once.

Here are some typical examples of categories. Note that the category titles are just one or two words that are descriptive enough that everyone knows what he or she means.

Sales

- Prospecting
- Making Presentations
- Proposal Development
- Follow-up

Manufacturing

- Packaging
- Loading
- Safety
- Quality

Proficiency Statements

Within each category, there are around three to seven statements. If there are only one or two statements, they probably should be combined with another category. If there are more than ten statements, it's a good idea to create a new category and split this one up. As I've said before, there are about 30 to 60 statements in a proficiency definition. If there are more than 60 statements, check to see if there are just describing steps in a task and need to be moved up a level. "Press the Start Button" is an important part of a task but it's not a proficiency. If there are less than 30 proficiency statements, they may be too all-encompassing and need to be split up.

The place to start when building a proficiency definition is to look for documents and measures that will help. This includes mission statements, KPIs, performance appraisals, task lists, training manuals, Standard Work, and SOP documents.

The next step is to lay out the major tasks within each category. Here are some major tasks:

- Building a marketing plan
- Developing proposals
- Implementing a daily care plan
- Performing preventive maintenance

The idea is to work at a high enough level so that you are not recreating the procedure manual or steps within a task such as pushing the start button or logging off at the end of the days. Some proficiency statements are at a macro level such as:

- Develops a client base of more than 100 customers
- Follows health and safety procedures when implementing the daily care plan

These larger proficiencies usually relate to a business or performance goal for that job. Attaining this proficiency will require becoming proficient in smaller ways as well. As you evaluate proficiency statements, you may see that some are too small or too general and they can be combined with others. For example, there could be a safety category with several safety proficiency statements. One option is to break this apart and add the safety component to other proficiency statements. For example, if there is a statement about operating a machine press, you would add a safety standard there.

In the beginning, I used to get the Learning Path team together to work on a proficiency definition. It took about six to eight hours, and everyone said their head hurt when it was done. A great deal of the time was spent arguing about the right numbers to use, whether it's 20 a week or 30. It always showed there was little consensus on what people should do and how. Again, brainstorming from a blank whiteboard is not very effective, and it wastes time.

Instead, what I do today is conduct an interview with each of the stakeholders and experts. It's usually 10 to 15 people. I ask them about what people do and how they are measured. I ask them about how long it takes to become proficient as well. From this, I can create a draft proficiency definition with the Learning Path team. The team then looks at correcting any mistakes, adding what's missing, rewriting statements, or tossing some out. This takes about half the time but ends up with a better result. It reduces the amount of Aspirin needed.

Milestones

The concept of a proficiency milestone is based on the fact that you don't become proficient in everything all on the final day. Employees who become proficient in a few tasks in the first weeks will probably be performing those tasks at a much higher level when the Learning Path ends six months later.

Let's examine a manufacturing Learning Path. An operator could become fully proficient with the packaging machine at the end of the second week. However, learning the other machines might take another twelve weeks. After two weeks, this employee can work on the packaging machine while the rest of the Learning Path continues.

In other cases, a salesperson could be proficient selling product line A in 2 months and product line B in eight months. A bank loan officer could take loan applications in six weeks but not make their first loan for eighteen months.

Where the milestone dates lie is easier to determine after mapping out a Learning Path. You will know where the training starts and stops for each proficiency statement. If the training activities include all of the practice and coaching, the end date of the training is close to the proficiency milestone date. As you upgrade a Learning Path, milestone dates will change as learning activities are moved around and resorted. Over time, good measurement data can be used to determine more exact milestone date.

The proficiency definition becomes the assessment tool for a Learning Path. However, there isn't one big assessment at the end. Instead, there are periodic and planned assessments at milestone dates. At a milestone date, the only passing score is 100%. Otherwise, the training needs to continue and then reassessed.

A quick word about proficiency statements that have a time component. If it states something like per week or per month, proficiency can't be achieved in one week or one month. Statistically, it takes three data points to make a trend. With this in mind, per week means a minimum proficiency is reached at the end of three weeks.

Evaluation

For each proficiency statement, there needs to be a way to evaluate or measure proficiency. If the statement is not observable or measurable, it's not a proficiency statement. It's something else. Most proficiency statements will have some numbers such as sales, error rate, or production. The evaluation method involves finding those reports, documents, or other sources where those numbers are captured and reported. This might be a weekly production or sales report.

Some proficiency statements can be evaluated by expert observation. Experts are pretty good at knowing success when they see it. Checklists or documents such as standard work or SOPs can support those expert observations. Since these documents are usually generated by the experts, they make an agreed upon standard for proficiency. In a well-documented Learning Path, there should be notes about how the employee did during each learning activity including weekly reviews.

At the start of a Learning Path project, experts often don't agree on every aspect of proficiency. Often building the proficiency statement with the team builds a consensus that these experts will support.

One of the challenges of this type of evaluation is that you are looking for 100%, getting most of it isn't good enough. If no one is getting 100%, it's a clue that the definition of proficiency was a goal and not a proficiency statement. The Learning Path is ensuring everyone gets to a level that others have reached in the past.

In the end, you can't speed up time to proficiency without a robust proficiency definition. In fact, it's almost impossible to measure it without this definition. The first proficiency definition will become the baseline for time to proficiency. The time it takes for employees to meet this definition is much further out than simply when the training ends. However, the goal is to reduce time to proficiency and not necessarily time in the classroom or in front of a computer screen. To easily get a 30% reduction in time to proficiency, you have to start with a realistic assessment of when the learner reaches proficiency.

Top Performers

Becoming a top performer can take months or years. The more complex and specialized the job, the longer it takes. If you are in little league, you would expect a level of proficiency that included hitting a major league curveball. In fact, a beginner would be years away from this goal and may never get there.

Therefore, it's critical to set different levels of proficiency based on required levels of performance for the job. Set one level for new employees and another for more advanced employees on their way to top performer.

In manufacturing environments. Instead of having one level of proficiency for an operator there might be three or four. The first level includes operating safely and meeting minimum production goals. In the second, level the operator meets high-level production goals and takes on additional responsibilities. At the third level, the operator can now handle very specific and more complex problems.

As a result, the training for a level one operator doesn't include all of the special problems and complex situations. However, that is the focus on level three training.

In some environment, producing top performers isn't always the goal. Instead, it's a matter of getting everyone performing at the same level.

Here's an example, I've always said that call centers are like Dairy Queens®. Dairy Queen® has been serving soft serve ice cream since the forties, and they are everywhere. My experience with Dairy Queen® is kind of unusual. When I was in grade school, my father developed an ulcer. The treatment for an ulcer was to have some type of dairy every hour. My father's solution was to stock our freezer with Dairy Queen® Dilly Bars. This is a disk portion of vanilla ice on a stick covered with chocolate. I became very popular in the neighborhood with a freezer full of Dilly Bars. The only rule in the house was that no one could eat the last Dilly Bar.

So how does this relate to a call center? Dairy Queens® used to staff up for the summer with teenage help. The one I went to all the time would have ten or twelve employees running around when it got busy. There were very good with the basics. If you wanted a vanilla cone, you were in good shape. If you want to have something more exotic, you had to wait for the one kid who knew how to make everything. In fact, you could see everyone standing around the one kid as he or she made a banana split.

In a call center, there is always someone who knows everything and can solve your problem. You just have to hope you get that person. Even when you get to the supervisor level, there is one supervisor who has the answers. This is a direct result of how agents are training and when they were trained.

If you want to see this in action, try this approach the next time you work with a call center. When you have an issue, instead of arguing or asking for a supervisor, simply hang up and dial again. Usually, after you call about five times, you will finally get the kid, and your problem will be solved.

Not too long ago, I called about a technical issue with my phone. After four agents and one supervisor, I got the kid. Not only did he recognize and solve the problem without putting me on hold, but he also recognized how I could save about $30 a month on my bill.

In this type of environment, the goal is not to create top performers but to create a consistent level of performance, so there is little difference from one call to the other.

Finally, in this chapter, we explored how to describe proficiency in a way that's observable and measurable. Proficiency becomes the finish line for training so that we know and see it when we get there.

CHAPTER 7:

A Process Approach to Learning

About ten years ago, I was working with a major bank on their new hire training. It started with a fourteen-week program for a new hire group of twenty. That's a lot of training! So we decided to map it out on the floor. The room was huge, maybe seventy-five feet long. I thought it was plenty of space, but it turned out to be barely enough. Together, we laid out each classroom activity followed by all of the follow-up training and coaching. We wrote the names of these activities on a large file card and placed it in order on the floor.

When done, we all stood back and took a look at what we had done. You literally had to walk from one end of the room to the other. The visual impact was stunning. To a person, everyone had the same reaction, "This is the craziest thing we ever saw." The first half of the room covered the formal training. It was filled with tests and games, some lectures, demonstration, and practice. The first few weeks of training was all done by the training group in the classroom. The next quarter of the room was dedicated to on-the-job training that for the most part fixed all the problems created by the first group.

You probably guessed this by now, the final portion of the room was the training done by supervisors who spent their time fixing what the first two groups did. Almost eight weeks of this training was spent retraining and fixing problems.

What I came away with from this experience with an appreciation for the value of having people visualize their training rather than just giving it to them on a piece of paper or spreadsheet. As you look at it, some issues and problems jump right out and demand to be fixed.

Today, instead of using the floor, I use the wall and large sticky notes. Instead of having the team brainstorm what today's training looks like, I do some upfront research and post my best guess on the wall and then let the team react. This shortens the process by hours, and the quality of the review is significantly better. The team is better at finding what's missing or what doesn't make sense then they are at creating everything from scratch.

When preparing the current Learning Path, write on each sticky note is the title of the activity and approximately how long it takes. Since this is a current Learning Path, it's usually obvious what everything is. The sticky notes don't need to have a big description.

With all the sticky notes on the wall, I've noticed a common look for most current Learning Paths. First, the majority of the learning activities are jammed into the first few days and the first few weeks. You can imagine the minimal amount of this training that is actually remembered or used by the time the training has been completed. The typical reaction is to spread out the learning activities in a more realistic manner.

One of the challenges of mapping out a current Learning Path is that there are often many paths instead of one path. Unfortunately, we don't need multiple paths; we need one good and consistent path. Through a process of discussion and negotiation, a best practice current path can be developed. As a result, a high degree of variability has been eliminated. We can now accelerate one path instead of ten. This is a core principle of process improvement, first, define or map the process and then look for ways to improve the process.

Most current Learning Paths have a huge mystery period. The current training might be 14 weeks, but proficiency may not be reached until 26 weeks. That's a big gap in the path. It's one place we know we can improve by shrinking the mystery period.

The final discovery from mapping out the path is that new learning activities need to be added while others need to be deleted. Walk the length of the path with the proficiency definition in hand and ask, does this path get to this destination? Are there missing activities? Are there activities on the path that no longer add any value, may be outdated or are just time killers?

Mapping a current Learning Path is a very simple activity that doesn't take much time but will reveal a fairly long list of ways to make the training better and faster. It's not uncommon to come up with a list of 50 to 100 improvement ideas. Once the improvement ideas have been incorporated into the current Learning Path, you now have a new accelerated Learning Path that should now be at least 30% faster. This Learning Path provides a big picture and structure that makes the most sense.

One of the usual suspects on a Learning Path is what I call the parade of departments. This can last a few days or a few weeks. A new employee is exposed to every department usually in an hour PowerPoint presentation. Sometimes the departments just wing it. It's done this way because it's convenient for the department heads. They get to check it off their list. Probably resulted in more sleeping and less learning at this time.

As any inventor would say, "There's got to be a better way." First, this isn't training or at least with less than a 5% retention rate; it's not very good training. Even something as simple as no more than one of these sessions per day would help.

What I truly like about the approach of treating learning as a process and mapping out that process is that I can tell people that it's not problem-solving, it's process improvement. Instead of telling people they're doing things wrong or that they have big problems, you get to say that this is where we are, and now we are going to get better. In fact, process improvement means continuous improvement. Instead of perfection, we are seeking improvement. This provides an opportunity for the organizations that are doing a good job on their training to get even better. Ironically, it's like everything else in that people who are good at something are more likely to work on improvement than those aren't good at all. The best always seem to have the most coaches and are more willing to take feedback.

With a current, agreed upon Learning Path staring us in the face, it's time to put a foot on the accelerator. It's okay to start anywhere because many of the improvements needed will be obvious. However, the concept of getting the sequence right is so critical that I've given it an entire chapter.

Let's start by working with our proficiency definition. There isn't going to be a learning activity for each proficiency. That's because there may be a series of learning activities for each proficiency statement and we may be teaching more than one proficiency at a time. Producing something without error can be taught along with reaching a certain level of output. Both are going to require a demonstration activity with follow-up and coaching activities.

Therefore to improve the Learning Path, the first question to ask is, "Does this Learning Path get us to proficiency or is it happening in some other way, or not at all?" Each learning activity should directly relate to one or more proficiency statements.

This activity helps us double check our proficiency definition. It's possible that there isn't enough time, practice, or coaching to reach the proficiency level that was set. Either this needs to be accounted for in the Learning Path, or the proficiency statement needs to change. If the current Learning Path leads to handling ten calls per hour, but proficiency is 15, there needs to be something added. The approach of "Here's your training; we hope you get better" needs to be eliminated.

If I Ran the World

Few things work out as planned. There are always some activities that can only be done when something else happens. You can't unjam a machine until it's jammed. You can't see a proposal presentation until there's a proposal to present. This is where tolerance of ambiguity comes in.

The best approach is to create a Learning Path in the "If I ran the world" mode. Activities are laid out where the experts predict work the best. Then as problems arise, you make adjustments. You can't plan for a power outage, but you can make adjustments and work on power outages when they happen.

Activity Descriptions

For every activity on a Learning Path, the detail is provided in an activity description. The activity description provides an overview or purpose of the activity and step-by-step instructions. Three different types of activity descriptions cover the entire range of training in a Learning Path. First, there are activity descriptions for formal training. These activity descriptions recap, review, and link to training such as workshops, e-learning, and webinars. For example, if an e-learning lesson is on the Learning Path it gets an activity description that includes the following:

- Overview
- Directions on how to accesses or sign up for the course
- Directions for debriefing the activity including any
  follow-up discussions

The second type of learning activity covers the informal learning including hands-on, experiential and social learning. This type of learning activity provides step-by-step instructions for this activity. This is spelled out in detail in the chapter on making informal training formal.

The third type of learning activity is used for review and assessment of progress along the path. This is best looked at by the following discussion of coaches and mentors.

Coaches and Mentors

Who is there to help you succeed? I like the idea that someone should be in charge or making sure an employee gets through their Learning Path successfully and on time. This could be a manager, supervisor, lead, trainer, or someone at a level who can make adjustments to the Learning Path and arrange for additional learning activities. A coach or mentor is a different role than that of the person doing the training.

Here's what the coach or mentor does. At the start of every Learning Path, there is an activity called, "Starting Your Learning Path." It's a great title. This is an hour or two meeting when the coach or mentor explains the proficiency definition and how it's used for evaluation. It includes walking through the Learning Path and talking about key activities. This is also the time to talk and how the Learning Path is scheduled. The coach or mentor and the employee discuss and agree on how and when they work together.

The second part of the coach or mentor's role is to check on progress. Review meetings are set and scheduled. Most Learning Paths will do this once a week at the end of the week. As long as it's consistent, it doesn't matter exactly when it's done. At this review meeting, the coach or mentor asks these questions:

- What learning activities did you complete this week?
- What do you have left over that needs to be scheduled next week?
- What went well?
- What was difficult or challenging?

Second, the coach or mentor checks on progress against the proficiency definition. This check should focus on any proficiency statements that should have been completed based on its milestone date. This might require a review of the employee's work or other measures specified in the proficiency definition. If the employee isn't proficient at this point, the coach or mentor needs to redo some of the activities or determine how to give more time for practice and feedback. The coach or mentor needs to decide if this employee is ready to move on.

Once an accelerated Learning Path is in place, it may change the proficiency milestone dates. First, when proficiency speeds up, these milestones occur sooner. Second, you may have completely changed the order. A learning activity that was at the start of the Learning Path might be moved a few weeks later.

As a result, certain milestone dates have to be flipped. Keep in mind that after the first few times the Learning Path is used, these dates will become more accurate. This is part of a continuous process of looking at the proficiency definition and Learning Path together. As one changes, the other ones usually changes as well.

This chapter presented a way to treat learning as a process and transform it into a very usable Learning Path. Remember that this isn't a way to reach perfection or necessarily solve the problem. It's a way to work on improvement. The Learning Path connects to the proficiency by identifying the fastest way to get to proficiency.

Just a final note, working on learning as a process is a creative process that brings out new ideas on what to put in, take out, combine, and move around. It doesn't always have to be neat, clean and organized. In the end, you'll end up pulling everything back together, and it will be relatively easy to put into action.

CHAPTER 8

Sequence, Sequence, Sequence

Since a Learning Path is a sequence of learning activities from start to proficiency, getting the sequence right has a huge impact on how long it takes to complete the path. There are general rules to sequencing activities, but sometimes the answer is unexpected and comes from the creativity of those doing the job. Here are a couple of examples:

Finding the Right Sequence

The first time I saw sequencing make a big difference was when I was working with health aides providing residential care for severely disabled. This was part of a grant project for Minnesota Job Skills. New health aides received very traditional training which started with the required training mandated by the State of Minnesota. In the first 72 hours for all healthcare workers, needed to be training on basic topics such as CPR. Then for the new few weeks, the training went through about a dozen other healthcare topics such as hygiene, meal preparation, and IV therapy.

Once the formal training was over, the health aides were sent out to the residential houses to work with their supervisor. Most of the training was hands-on.

Hands-on training was different in every house partly because residents had a wide range of disabilities. Some were ambulatory while others weren't. Some had limited speech or couldn't talk, while other were very social some were very anti-social. Learning how to deal with a very social resident who could walk was very different from a very anti-social quadriplegic. As a result, it could take nine months to a year to become proficient.

After batting ideas around for half a day, the house managers came up with a great idea. What if instead of training everything by topic, training was rearranged by type of resident. A new health aide would be assigned to start working with a resident who had very basic needs. The health aide would then learn from the managers each of the daily care requirements until they became proficient for that type of resident.

While the aide was learning at this level, they would go through an hour or so each morning in more formal training. This spread the dozen or so topics over several weeks rather than back to back. It became possible to shorten this type of technical training by splitting it up into levels. For example, an aide would first learn how to help someone with showering who was fully ambulatory. Later, the aide would revisit showering for someone in a wheelchair.

After completing level 1 or patient 1, the health aide would be moved to the next resident based on difficulty. The aide wouldn't move to the next level until he or she had mastered the daily requirements for that patient. After working with four different patients, the health aide was fully trained to work with any resident.

Over time, this company has revised their Learning Path, making the training and the sequence even better. Time to proficiency has been reduced from more than nine months to about 60 days. The initial turnover problem all but disappeared.

Turnover is a critical problem and is very typical everywhere. Almost all turnover occurs in the first ninety days. Employees find that the work isn't what they thought it would be, they can't get along with their coworkers, they don't like their boss, or something better comes along. Working in this type of healthcare isn't for everyone. Getting more exposure to the job earlier helps new hires to make the decision to quit or stay in the first week rather than waiting for six months.

To progress quickly, the health aide needed to get help from other more experienced aides. However, other health aides resisted giving this type of help until the new hire had become "useful." In other words, the new health aide needed to be doing real work that helped others with some of the more basic tasks. When sequencing a Learning Path, it's a good idea to put in ways to make employees useful from the start.

This Learning Path didn't require building new training but instead advanced quickly by getting the sequence right. The new training that was added involved structuring the hands-on training in the houses and using the proficiency definition as the assessment tool to know when to move the aide to the next level.

As a side note, one of the frustrations of working in this type of environment is dealing with government regulations which have good intent but create problems. One of these regulations was the requirement to have a six-week meal plan. Sounds good but, no two meals could be repeated. That's six weeks of completely different meals. Now think about how you eat. Do you eat a different breakfast every day or do you basically eat the same thing? It's great to have meals that are nutritionally sound, but people have to be willing to eat it? Brussel sprouts might be good nutrition, but not if they are in the garbage can.

The meal plan becomes a big challenge when health aides have limited cooking experience. Because of the available workforce around this business, new employees came are from a wide range of cultures. As a result, they were often unfamiliar with many of the dishes on the menu. Trying to make something you've never eaten before is challenging. I remember one aide made a dish she called, 'weenie O's. Basically, it was Spaghetti O's with chopped up hotdogs.

In many cases, do the best you can with required training like this. It gets very expensive and time-consuming to try and get laws and regulations changed. You just have to assume the training won't stick and you will have to do it again the right way.

Simple to Complex, Easy-to-Hard

Three principles in this example can be applied to most Learning Paths. First, lining up all the topics one after the other is an easy way to teach, but it's not a very effective way to learn. Second, when possible, it's better to line up the path by real work from simple to complex. In other words, get good at something before moving on. Third, look for ways to make the employee useful so that others will be more willing to coach or mentor the new employee.

Here's a second example of sequencing that's fairly typical of most manufacturing. Have you ever seen how insulation is made? When I saw it, I think the words I used were, "This is cool!" It starts with sand being loaded into a furnace. The heat then creates a molten glass type substance which goes into something that looks like a giant cotton candy machine. The raw materials are spun into fiberglass and exit as insulation. It then goes down the line where it's cut to length, rolled and packaged.

One idea was to teach this job by stations from front to back starting with loading sand. Then move to the next station and continue all the way to packaging. In this middle of this discussion, a lead operator stood up and said, "This is totally nuts, you can't teach it this way." He said that what you realize if you start training at the beginning of the process, your mistakes create problems for everyone after that step. What you need to do is start by loading pallets after the insulation is bagged and then work your way up the line. Keep in mind that failing to load the pallets correctly, won't shut down the line.

The idea of becoming useful earlier transferred nicely to manufacturing. In any manufacturing plant, there is work new employees can do without a lot of training. Most of these are in the area of housekeeping or maintenance. As a result, this Learning Path team created a list of basic tasks. They would teach these tasks in the first few days and then anytime the new employee wasn't in training, they would be assigned to do one or more tasks from the list. When a new employee is willing to do some cleanup work or pitch in to help, it's looked upon very favorably by coworkers.

Another example involves training insurance salespeople to sell corporate health and benefits programs. This is a very complex job that can take years to learn. The team came up with the thought that it's hard to teach everything to every new salesperson before they could start selling. It's just too much stuff, and it would never stick. They decided to break up their Learning Path by customer type. They defined each customer type by numbers of employees and types of products they might use. It came down to about four customer types.

On one end of customer spectrum were those small companies usually less than 50 employees where the decision maker was usually the owner. These companies buy very basic plans, and it's usually easy to get into seeing a decision-maker.

On the other end of the spectrum were very large companies with over 2000 employees who will be self-funding. The team said that talking to a company about self-funding is something they wouldn't want a new employee to do for more than two years. I think you can start to see where this is going. On their Learning Path, all the training about self-funding doesn't start for almost two years. It's a waste of time and effort to do this in the first year.

The new Learning Path for these health and benefits salespeople is now sequenced by customer type. How to sell to level 1 customers and level 1 products and services is arranged around making of join calls to these types of customers. The initial prospecting and sales plan focuses on these customers. Three or four months later, they start training on the next level.

Just like the other two examples, the training sequence finds a way to go from easy to hard and simple to complex. Get good at something before trying to get good at everything. They all had a task or two that a new employee could do during downtime. The salespeople could always work on their prospecting list or making prospecting calls.

Yet another example comes from the call center world. I've worked in more than twenty call centers, and this one is very typical. The existing training consisted of four weeks of classroom training. Week one focused on the computer system and basic product information. The second week provided more in-depth product training. The third week focused on the different types of calls and including classroom practice. The final week combined more call training with beginning to take live calls. After the formal training, agents were assigned to a supervisor and work team. The agent received additional coaching for about two weeks, and then they were on their own.

The question was raised, "Do you need to know everything about everything before you take live calls." The answer was "No, you could route calls so you could take order related calls and not have to handle billing calls." The first thing the team did was create a process map of the different types of calls. It ended up that there were five major types of calls. The team then put them in a sequence that made it possible to teach them one at a time.

Today, there are five steps in their Learning Path. Each step is one call type and includes the computer, product, and process for that call. They practice in the classroom and take live calls until they reach a level of proficiency. Then they go back and learn the next call. Often call centers get short staffed and have to put trainees on to the floor to fill in. This made it possible to put trainees out on the floor in an emergency who could take certain types of calls without creating problems.

These are all good examples, but some people say the best learning comes from bad examples. One of the worst examples of getting the sequence wrong happened with a very large mortgage company. By the way, they are out of business now. The company felt that all those taking loan applications and underwriting needed to know all of the mortgage terms. There were more than one hundred of these terms. The training department got the idea that the best way to teach mortgage terms was to teach them alphabetically. As a result, new employees went through three days of some of the most painful training I've seen. After hours of evening study, almost everyone passed the test. But no one knew how any of this applied to their jobs, and most couldn't remember all the terms a few weeks later.

Just-in-Time

The concept of just-in-time learning has been floating around for a while. It means different things to different people, but it's useful to consider when looking at sequence. Just-in-time could mean having access to training or training materials when you need them. Knowledge and learning management systems (LMS) often make this promise.

I like to look at just-in-time a little differently. It's the concept that the distance in time between learning something and using it needs to be as short as possible. Here's an example, you are working in a manufacturing plant that makes its product by combining chemicals in large vats. This example works if you want to say we are just making beer. The vats need to be cleaned from time to time. However, because of the fumes, you need to wear a respirator along with some other protective equipment.

When you went through safety training in your first week, you learned how to use the respirator. Now six weeks later, you're going into the vats for the first time.

Your chances of remembering how to use the respirator are fairly small. This is the point where most companies have to retrain them how to use the respirator safely. For me, just-in-time training means you plan to clean out the vats on day 42 and in the morning of day 42, you do respirator training.

In each of the examples in this chapter, there was an element of just-in-time training. It means that training is broken up into smaller bits and then aligned with immediate practice and feedback. One client told me that he got the idea of Learning Paths when he saw that instead of teaching safety and then the job, we were teaching how to do each part of the job safely.

I have found that just-in-time applies to coaching as well. Coaching everything at the same time is impossible. It's more confusing than helpful. Instead, focus on one thing at a time and get better at it before moving on. Saying, "Here are the 10 things I want you to remember" doesn't work as a coaching method.

So here's a quick recap of the getting the sequence right. First, the sequence can make a big difference without spending a lot of money. Moving learning activities around, combining some activities and breaking apart others doesn't take very much time. Second, the general rules of sequencing are to go from simple to complex and from easy to hard. Third, structure the training around how the job is done and try to get good at one thing before moving on to the next.

Finally, to get the sequence right ask the experts how they learned. When you give them the opportunity to think about it and be creative, they can come up with some surprising answers. They sometimes need to be pushed out of the box of the traditional, line up all the topics approach.

As you build your Learning Paths, they should look very different than a typical school curriculum, list of courses or training plan. It shouldn't be topic by topic. Instead, it should follow the logical sequence of the best way to learn the job with every part of it structured and detailed.

CHAPTER 9

Getting Technology Training Right

Microsoft Word came out in 1983. It's been a powerful tool and business standard ever since. That's why I'm always surprised that more people than not use it as a typewriter. I learned out to type on an old Royal Standard typewriter, so it's easy for me to spot the similarities. I see people space or tab over to center a title at the top of a document, and they hit the enter button until it makes a new page. When I do Learning Path projects, I often have to spend teaching people many of the basic features of Word, PowerPoint, and Excel. These are not hard programs to learn, and there is endless training available. The question is, why doesn't any of it stick?

Changing How People Work

Good software adds capabilities, makes work easier, and standardizes work output. However, it doesn't come with guidance on how to make a specific job or task easier. Learning happens when a user needs to do a specific task such as create a procedure manual or proposal in a specific way. Those who try to learn this on their own will often find ways to workaround a feature they don't know how to use. I can't tell you how many people want to put everything into Excel because they won't use tables in Word.

What complicates this problem is that most software has several ways to do the same operation. I can think of at least five different ways to cut and paste. However, I can only use one at a time. As a result, there aren't standard ways to get things done, so it's a free-for-all.

The issues are perhaps easier to see by looking at some of the bigger enterprise-wide software such as enterprise resource planning (ERP), CRM, (HRIS, or LMS. Each of these programs, when implemented correctly, is great, but there are roadblocks and pitfalls along the way.

From a training standpoint, it's important to recognize that each of these systems fundamentally changes the way people work. Like or not, everyone is going to have a new job.

I had an interesting experience with a customer relationship management program that illustrates the point. The client was going through training by the vendor on the system including learning all the bells and whistles and how the program was going to maximize the marketing effort.

The instructor was explaining how to create a custom email campaign. He said, "Now you just put your customer data in here." From the class, the question came, "Where is our customer data." The instructor said, "In the customer database." The participant then remarked, "You don't get it, we don't keep that kind of customer information. How can we get it?"

Historically, this company didn't capture most customer information. It wasn't part of their sales process. As a result, to make this new software work, the salesforce had to be retrained on asking better questions and capturing customer information so they could then use it in the software. It took about a year to get enough information to make the new database system valuable. If that question weren't raised, executives would be asking questions about why they invested in this software when no one used it.

Enterprise Software

I've worked on several ERP implementations and here is a situation that is very common. The instructor was talking about how the system would deliver real-time information to help managers improve their budgets. A hand came up from the audience with the comment, "We don't do budgets." In order to make that great data useable, the company had to go back, install a budgeting process, and then teach managers to use the new data to do their budgeting.

ERP systems generate massive amounts of data and reports. There can be as many as a 1000 reports. Unfortunately, no one can use 1000 reports. They have to be selective and use the ones that are most meaningful to them. This requires examining the job and determining what information and reports will be used in this job. This is not as simple as it sounds because it may be a complete job redesign. Just knowing how to enter data and run reports isn't the training that is needed.

Bottom line, the starting point for new software needs to be looking at how it will change the way people work. At the start of this process, many companies realize that they don't know what people are doing today, so it's unclear what needs to be changed. One of the by-products of a Learning Path project is that it becomes very clear what people are doing, how they are doing it, and what are the expectations. When you have an agreed upon definition of proficiency, it's then possible to see how proficiency might change or improve using the software.

Legacy Systems

Along with how jobs change, I've found that most companies have three computer systems. The first is the old legacy system. The old legacy is where most of the historical data lies. It's costly and expensive to migrate it to the new system. The second is the one in use today. This is the one everyone uses and provides the most comfort. There are plenty of problems, but everyone is used to it.

Finally, the new system is the one coming in. It's going to fix everything. It's not fully functional yet, but it's on the way. I worked with one large company where the new system never seemed to be finished. They kept promising any week now for almost two years. I've seen companies that use a dual screen to make it easy to see information from the legacy system while using the current system.

It's challenging to try and change three systems at once. However, this isn't a training problem; it's a problem for IT. As they launch new software and updates, they have to be more aware of what it means for their users. They need to see how employees are using the systems today to be aware of how it's going to change how people work in the future.

Integrated Approach

Now, let's turn to how technology is usually taught and why it doesn't stick. There has always been a very tall wall between hard and soft skills or technical and non-technical training. They are taught independently by two different sets of instructors. However, there isn't a separation between the two on-the-job. While it's more difficult to combine the two as an instructor or designer, it's much harder to figure out how to combine them on the job.

When you watch a call center agent on a call, you will see that the computer system is used in conjunction with talking with the customer. The agent is finding and entering information while having a productive conversation with the customer. The agent will navigate from screen to screen based on the conversation. Therefore, instead of teaching navigating and accessing information separately from the flow of the conversation, they need to be taught together.

This approach has the effect of streamlining what the agent is taught. Instead of learning all of the different ways to access information, agents only learn the one they are going to be using. I've sat through many software training courses, where the agent learns operation one way, and then when they get to their station, someone then teaches them all the shortcuts and how things are done. One way to cut training time is just to teach what people are going to use. This relates directly back to the story about Microsoft word at the beginning of the chapter.

As you combine, technical and non-technical training, it changes the sequence of the approach. Instead of teaching all of the software at once, it gets broken into small bits that align with specific parts of the job. For example, in a call center, you might teach order taking as a first step. Then only the part of the computer system that relates to order taking is taught along with the order taking process. Training transfers to the job by adding practiced until everything sticks. Then go on to a next step such as billing calls.

Consider how you might teach a CRM. One thing salespeople learn to do is generate a prospecting list. This activity should then be combined with how to enter the prospect list in the system and how to access and use the list. Everything about sales call planning is taught after this. The guiding principle is to always think about what parts of the software are going to be used and how they can be applied on the job. Then teach and practice that part of the job before going to the next step.

This chapter focused on technology and the best way to teach technology. It took a high-level look at how to use technology to train. Technology is changing rapidly, and it's a great idea to keep current with new products and trends. Always keep in mind that technology isn't something separated from the job. It has to be integrated. Without this integration, it won't be used the way it should be, or to the extent that it needs to be.

CHAPTER 10:

When Good Isn't Good Enough

"Good morning, this is John Jones, your pilot. We'll be flying down to Miami today. The weather in Miami is 85 and sunny, and we don't expect any turbulence in route. By the way, I'm very excited about flying today. I just graduated from flight school with a 90% score on my landing test. That's an A in anybody's book."

Ninety percent is a good score on any test. However, in this case, it's simply not good enough. I'm sure you can imagine all the passengers pushing to the exits to try and get off this plane. There are many examples of jobs where anything less than 100% isn't good enough. Do you expect your pharmacist to get your prescription filled 100% correctly? Getting it wrong could be deadly.

In some jobs, even small mistakes have huge consequences. I worked in a factory where they made resins. Resins are a result of a chemical reaction caused by mixing various components in large kettle-like vats. Adding chemicals in the wrong order in wrong amounts can cause a runaway reaction that can quickly burn the plant to the ground. There is simply no room for error.

Passing Score

While these may seem like extreme examples, there are others that are common and every day. Imagine talking with someone in a call center. They've been training for a few days to as much as eight weeks. Their passing score is often no more than 75%. A good solid C. What this means is that 25% of what they know is wrong and the rest they can't remember. The company tries to minimize the effects by installing processes, scripts, and procedures that the agents can follow step by step. That's why when you call back and talk to someone else; they start all over again. But, with running businesses that use a call center, they are constantly giving out wrong information that leads to more errors, returns, and unhappy customers.

Do you ever wonder why there is so much indecision when several cars approach an uncontrolled intersection or even one with a four-way stop? Some will push to go first while others wait until the intersection clears. All of these people passed their driver's test, and yet this situation is commonplace. One answer is that it only takes 75% to pass most driver's tests. For many people, this falls into the missing 25%.

One of the challenges for self-driving cars is that human drivers don't know all the rules or play by the rules. Some people drive as if traffic rules were suggestions and not the law. While we learn to deal with this as we drive, we also do a lot of swearing. I wonder if the self-driving cards will be able to scream out, "Where did you get your driver's license?"

Testing

As knowing and doing are not the same, testing for knowledge versus performance is different. A great deal of knowledge testing is done through multiple choice tests. There is a question with three to five possible responses. The way tests are written, two or three responses are written so if you know anything about the topic, you can eliminate them. Then there are two responses which are similar with only slight differences. A good test taker can quickly boil down the choices to two, and then there's a 50/50 chance of being right. On the other hand, questions are missed because the question was written in an ambiguous way, or if you take them too literally, you will get them wrong.

The main advantage of multiple choice and true/false tests is that they are easy to score especially with a large number of test takers. In fact, they can all be machine scored in seconds. Multiple choice doesn't relate to how the information they learned will be used on the job. On the job, when a customer asks technical questions, a series of choices doesn't pop up. You have to know the right answer and know it quickly. Answering rapid fire questions is a much better test.

Reality is harder than paper and pencil tests because having the answer in your head is easier than being able to put the answer into words. This is a key point for any position that has direct customer contact. Saying the words, rehearsing the words, and repeating the words is the only way to become fluent with the answers. This is one of the main reasons why knowledge testing isn't always predictive of on the job performance. In the contact centers I've worked in, I've seldom seen a test online or in the classroom were predictive of on-the-job performance.

Finally, memorizing a lot of information for a test isn't the best way to ensure retention of the knowledge. Students usually remember best what they use. The more time between knowledge acquisition and putting into practice, the more likely the information will be forgotten. Our pilot who needs to land the plane 100% of the time, can't be relied on always to remember what to do. That's why he has detailed checklists for everything and goes through them for each landing.

So what's a better way to look at testing and evaluation especially when the only real passing score is 100%? Here's one way. There is "real power" in evaluation by observation by an expert. I've had years of experience with this in many different settings. When you watch and listen to travel agents take calls and book trips, you can see a significant difference between someone who is just average and a top agent. It's obvious. Here's some of what you will see:

- There is a consistent flow and process for the call that seems natural for the agent
- The agent finds information quickly by moving from screen to screen without backtracking
- The agent sounds confident in the recommendations they make
- Now watch an experienced a top machine operator in a manufacturing plant. Here's what you will see:
- They work in an organized and disciplined manner with little-wasted effort
- They are wearing the correct protective equipment, and they are following safety standards
- They take quick and appropriate action something goes wrong

Observing Performance

I've been told that I watch way too many cooking shows. However, from these shows, I learned all about mise en place. Mise en place is a French expression for having everything in its place. It's about doing all the prep work properly and being ready to cook. Top chefs focus on their mise en place, so they aren't running around back and forth to get things done. Focusing on mise en place leads to a safe work environment that likely meets health and safety standards.

Think of all the other jobs and work areas where the concept of mise en place applies. I worked with one group of truck mechanics who thought this was perfect for organizing the garage and each mechanic's workspace.

In observing workplace performance, there are often just a few key factors to look for that tell the entire story. I was working in a plant that produced fiber cement siding. I asked, how can you tell if someone is proficient in their job? What can you see? I was surprised by this answer, "All you have to do is look at the operator's work area at the end of the day. If it's neat, organized and clean, you know they are doing a great job. Unless you were doing your work right, you would never have time to do this type of cleaning and organizing."

Beyond observation, the numbers tell a big part of the story. Most jobs have a few key activities that can be measured and tracked. Jobs in sales, production, and even service have measures such as:

- Sales and profitability
- Output per hour
- Number of calls taken
- Reject or scrap rate
- Customer satisfaction ratings

These are the same numbers the business looks at often referred to KPIs or key performance indicators. These are the same numbers that measure job performance and often appear on performance appraisals. They are something the business cares about a great deal. Today, enterprise software is used to keep track of these numbers and produce reports on a real-time basis. Therefore, they are good sources of this information.

There are two major downsides of using performance as a measure of training. First, training often isn't designed to take a learner from start to a set level of performance. That type of training needs to replicate the learning process with all the activities including practice, coaching, and experience. It's not uncommon for this type of training to take weeks, months, and in some cases years.

Second, it's just easier to hold a class or give an e-learning program and hope there is some long-term effect on performance. However, this presents the challenge of trying to connect training to results. A classic challenge is to try and connect a sales workshop to increased sales. There might be a change in sales after the class, at least in the short term. But was the workshop the cause or was it something else? To verify that it was the class, you would need to observe salespeople on calls and see if they were using their new skills and knowledge in the right way. It's difficult, but I don't think the training world is ready for double-blind studies.

Most workshops, webinars, and e-learning are promoted with a set of learning objectives that start with what the learner will be able to do after the training is done. In most cases, these objectives are way overstated. For example, "in this 2-hour webinar, you will learn how to apply the 7 secrets of building effective teams." I would guess that if you asked participants the next day to list the 7 secrets, they might remember 1 or 2. The reality is that it takes time and practice working with teams to learn to apply these concepts.

By focusing on using performance measures for training, forces the designer to focus on what happens after the class is over and what steps need to be taken to ensure transfer of what was taught to the job. Unfortunately, this leaves the realm of the training department and requires active involvement with others in the organization who may be resistant to being involved with training.

Organizations are continuously sending out new policies and procedures. When they request training on these policies and procedures what they mean is just to tell employees what they are now required to do. They haven't thought out how these policies and procedures will be implemented and how they change the way people work. As a result, these changes are often ignored until there is a crisis.

Employees need to be trained on how their jobs or the work they are doing is going to change and then get practice and feedback as these changes are made. It's a tradeoff between taking more time to do training versus more time on-the-job struggling with the change.

In looking at using performance measures, there is a difference between performance management and training. For the most part, performance management works with employees who are already trained in their jobs and works on improving that performance to reach higher and higher levels. However, training needs to focus on getting employees who aren't fully trained to a desired or required level of performance.

Typically, performance management evaluates performance on a rating scale. There isn't a possible 100% score. You can always get better. Training needs to look at this differently by setting a level of required performance. To pass, a learner needs to reach this level of performance. It's a 100% measure. This means that the required level of performance is achievable through training, and that anything below that level isn't acceptable. At the end of training instead of saying that 85% is okay, action needs to be taken to ramp up performance. This might mean more training, practice, or coaching.

By setting this type of performance measure for training, it's possible to identify those who aren't capable of doing this job. For example, some jobs require both speed and accuracy such as picking orders or filling prescriptions. If someone can't meet the minimum performance standard for these jobs, it might be time to help them find something different to do.

One of the benefits of looking at training this way is that you can front load learning activities to find out what learners can do early. If they aren't going to make it, you want to find out early so you can avoid the weeks or months of training time on someone who isn't going to be doing this job. In this case, early attrition is a good idea.

Finally, performance management uses goals and stretch goals. These goals challenge an employee to do better and are often related to bigger business goals. A goal of reaching a 1% or less scrap rate is okay even if no one has ever done it before. It's only a reasonable performance measure for training if this is a required level of performance that incumbents typically achieve.

I have found that when work is consistently measured and follows well-defined and documented systems and processes, training becomes much more effective. As a result of working on a more performance-based training approach, there is a side benefit of beginning to structure and document how work gets done. In a manufacturing plant, it's common to have work done in different ways by the day shift versus the night shift. In many cases, there isn't a benefit of one approach over another; they are just different. In working on building the training, a potential result is to develop a single best practice approach that both shifts use.

When we get a group of stakeholders together to work on training, we find that there isn't an agreement on what performance should be. Just like the differences in practices, this creates a great deal of variability. Working through these disagreements and setting common standards means that there is a greater chance that everyone will be happy with the training.

In the end, this chapter relates directly back to the principle that knowing and doing aren't the same. Focusing on knowledge leads to standard tests while doing leads to observation and performance-based test. Knowing doesn't guarantee transfer to the job while doing means that this transfer is a requirement. By using the proficiency definition as the assessment tool, this ensures that gaining a required level of performance is the most important part of the evaluation.

CHAPTER 11:

All Aboard

Onboarding has certainly been an important part of Learning Paths for brand new employees. Consider how soon you would be confident assigning a new employee to work with your most valued customers? When do you know a new employee is likely to stay and be a productive member of your team? When do you know a new employee can be trusted to work without constant supervision? This usually happens long before an employee is fully proficient.

New employees are a gamble. Even with the best hiring process, there's no guarantee of success. There are plenty of downsides to employees who are slow to fit in or who never fit in. Therefore, the goal of any successful onboarding process or program should be to get new employees up to speed and working with their team as fast as possible.

While there are many ways to speed up onboarding during pre-hire activities. Making good hiring decisions is just one. For the purposes of this discussion, let's limit onboarding from day one until you comfortably feel a new employee is fitting in and well on the way to hitting performance targets. This is different than time to proficiency or time to productivity which, for many jobs, is months if not years away. Think of onboarding more in terms of making a big impact in the critical first 30 to 90 days.

Often when companies start to build onboarding programs, they start by asking the questions: "What does the employee need to know?" and "Who does the employee need to meet?" As a result, there is brief orientation followed by either visits or presentations by department heads. While all of this may eventually be important, it's often confusing, boring, and not directly related to their job. When there is a formal new hire training program that last weeks or months, it can be a very long time before the new employee becomes integrated with the job.

This chart shows how orientation lasts only a few hours or weeks, while onboarding is more in depth but not a full Learning Path. A Learning Path goes all the way to proficiency and includes all of the necessary training, coaching, and experience. Think of onboarding as an important piece of a larger learning path.

To build an effective onboarding program, let's start by looking at the first few weeks on the job from a new employee's point of view. Fortunately, most employees start work highly motivated and eager to work. However, they are also apprehensive because this is a new situation with new people. This is true even when employees have done the same or similar job before. The success and speed of their onboarding will now depend on how well three questions are answered for this new employee. Can I really do this job? Do I really want this job? Will I fit in?

Interestingly, the employer will almost always share these three doubts. Imagine hiring a new manager. There are always concerns that this new employee will fit in with the team and begin to make rapid improvements. They may have been successful in their old company, but that was then. This is now.

If you're hiring salespeople, the clock is ticking until they can generate enough in sales to break even on your investment in them. For frontline employees in call centers or on the manufacturing floor, there are concerns about production, safety, errors and more.

So let's take each of these questions one at a time and explore what they mean and what to do about them.

Question 1: Can I Really Do This Job?

Call centers provide great examples of onboarding issues because of the large numbers of employees that come and go. Here is an interesting story of how this question affects new employees. In this call center, customer service agents take orders, answer questions, and process billing. Traditionally, they spent about six weeks in training, taking their first live calls in week four. Because of everything that new employees need to learn, even experienced agents had questions about whether they could do the job when they went live.

We discovered that these new agents didn't need to know everything about all calls, all the products and the complete computer system to take a simple order call. We rearranged their training so that they learned only about a simple order so that they could begin taking basic calls by day three. On day three, they spent a half day taking real calls with the help of a coach.

When they returned to class on day four, there was a collective sigh of relief. New agents all felt that the job wasn't as hard as they thought and they could do this job. Compared to a similar class on the old method, they finished two weeks earlier and had a significantly lower turnover. Those in the old method class, carried their anxiety all the way into week four.

With salespeople, the sink or swim method is very popular. With a little bit or no training, salespeople are sent out cold calling on their own. Here is your phone and the phone book. Good luck! Unfortunately, the result of this method is that it produces more sinkers than swimmers. Unprepared a new salesperson is dumped into the deep end. This means that anyone who would have survived with a little help or training fails or quits. It's a tough way to answer the question, "Can I do this job?"

New managers are faced with these doubts as well. The work team can have all sorts of issues and problems. They can even openly challenge the new managers. Can the manager establish a position of leadership quickly or not? That's the big question. In these cases, sometimes the manager quits or ends up replacing all the team members. Either way, it's an expensive proposition.

While there are several effective strategies for handling this question, here are the top three:

1. Get to work early

   You will never know how well new employees will perform until they start working. While they may not be able to do the entire job for some time, there is always something they can work on.

2. Find an early opportunity for success

   Confidence is built on success. Try to find a part of the job that can be mastered quickly, the sooner, the better. For salespeople, this might be calling on certain types of customers who are less complicated and friendlier. For managers, this might be holding well-structured meetings with their team.

3. Make training just-in-time

   Don't overload new employees with training especially if they won't need it immediately. Try to schedule training as close to the time it will be used as possible. When new employees go through weeks of initial training, a lot of it doesn't stick because it isn't immediately used. It becomes overwhelming and creates a loss of confidence and morale

Having the capability to do something isn't the same as performing a task, in all key situations, under pressure. As Mike Tyson said, "Everyone's got a plan until they get hit in the face." Good hiring practices will yield employees with a high likelihood of success and not a guarantee. Let's go on to the second question.

Question 2: Do I Really Want to Do This Job?

Human resources often does a great job selling potential new employees on the job and the company. However, when the realities of the job set in, these new employees can be disillusioned. Here are two examples of common situations that occur.

In collections call centers, at some point in the initial training, the lights go on for many agents, and they'd say, "So what you're saying is, you want me to call people at home during dinner and ask them for money, is that right?" A predictable percentage would say, "I'm not going to do that" and quit. The reality didn't hit them until they had a phone in their hand and were told to call. Having this epiphany after six weeks of training wasted a lot of time and effort.

Here's the other example. People often go into customer service thinking it's a job to help customers. After taking a call or two, you often hear, "All these customers do is call and complain. I don't want to do this." In the old days, customer service used to be the complaint department and attracted a little different type of person.

The bottom line is this. The sooner employees do real work with real customers, the sooner they can answer the question, "Do I really want to do this job?" The longer you wait, the more expensive it gets.

Here are the top three strategies for dealing with the question, "Do I really want this job?"

1. Preview a Day in the Life

   As early as possible, even pre-hire, let the new employee see real work on the job. A day of job shadowing is not a bad idea.

2. Establish the Daily Routine

   Get the new employee into the routine of the job on the first day if possible. If the new employee will be working on the second or third shift, then that's when the training should be scheduled. If you're in a manufacturing plant, start wearing personal protective equipment immediately.

3. Experience the Challenge

If the job requires taking calls from angry customers, new employees need to see and feel how they would react in those situations. If the new employee is providing care for disabled or sick patients, they need to meet and begin working with these patients.

Just because people need a job or think they want to work for your company, this doesn't mean that they won't change their minds. It can be a real emotional roller coaster as employees view themselves in this new role.

And finally, don't forget what employees hear when they start to explain what they do every day to their friends and family. What they thought was a good idea can quickly be shot down. Be ready and deal with this question as fast as you can. Now let's go on to the final question.

Question 3: Will I Fit In?

Working in a new company or work team is like being dropped into a new family. Not everyone is accepted immediately, and not everyone will fit in. You can expect some resistance and even hostility from current employees. This is especially true when a work team gets a new manager or supervisor.

I found an interesting slant to this issue when I was working with a company that provided residential care for severely disabled. They talked about how one of the biggest obstacles new employees had was gaining enough acceptance from the team so that the team would be willing to invest time training that person. What they talked about was not a date of being fully up to speed but rather a date at which a new employee became useful. So, in their onboarding plan, they teach new employees some basic "helping hand" tasks that are valuable to the team.

Here are a couple of common situations that you might want to avoid. The new employee is sent off for weeks of training. They won't get a desk, phone, or even place to sit until they get back. It will be some time before they meet their coworkers and supervisor. As a result, all through training, the question, "Will I fit in?" doesn't get answered.

Often, there is no real plan for new employee training. I've seen new employees assigned to read policy books or proposals for two to three weeks with little interaction with anyone. The message is that everyone else is too busy and when they get time, they will start training the new person.

Managers have a very short time to become assimilated or assume their leadership position. Everyone else is on pins and needles until this happens. Some of the best onboarding includes early team sessions where the new manager tries to hear, understand, and respond to the questions and concerns of the team.

I think all too often the method for getting people to work with each other is to put them together and see what results. It's a form of sink or swim. Here are three quick suggestions for answering, "Will I fit in?"

1. Early Introductions

    Make sure new employees meet and spend time with their managers and team members in the first few days.

2. Establish a Home Base

    Give new employees their phones, desks, emails, or other startup essentials of their job immediately.

3. Structure Early Interactions

    Don't leave it to chance. Create activities that make the new person valuable to the team members and alleviates any doubts they have about the new person.

Successful onboarding requires structure for the first 30 to 90 days. Doing a better job of onboarding, dramatically reduces turnover and helps to build a more productive work environment. Getting down to real work and the routine of the job early can make a big difference.

CHAPTER 12:

Making Informal Training Formal

This chapter explores in more detail the principle of making learning happen by design rather than by accident. There's a popular TV show called "Undercover Boss." The top person in the company takes on a disguise to see what it's like for a new person in the company. The boss is always failing at everything he or she tries. Usually, the boss is slow or makes too many errors. Everyone is ready to fire the boss.

The boss learns from more experienced employees or supervisors. They show the boss once or twice how to do something and then leave them alone for a while. Surprisingly, this method doesn't work, but they blame it on a lack of capability by the boss. The boss always feels demoralized.

Maybe they should have shown the boss how to do something three or four times. Maybe the experienced employee needed to stick around until the boss started to do the task right. Maybe there was a better way to give feedback and correction. Every show I watched, the experienced employee was making up the training as he or she went along. It's likely the training was different every time it was done. If the boss, hadn't been the boss, it would have been likely that he or she would have gotten frustrated and quit. Fortunately, he or she was the boss.

In the old days, salespeople were given a phone and a phone book and told just to start selling. The good ones would figure it out. Today, we no longer use phone books, but the training isn't any better. I remember a company that prepared their new software engineers to do consulting by letting them read the project book for two weeks. There really wasn't anything to learn, but it kept the new employee busy until there was something else for them to do.

I've always called the time between the end of formal training and full proficiency the "Mystery Period." Unfortunately, the mystery period is the time when there is the most learning. It's called the mystery period because it's uncertain what happens. It's unstructured, hit and miss, and highly variable. In the mystery period, there is excessive trial-and-error learning where the new employee makes the same mistakes as their predecessors. When we talk about reducing time to proficiency by at least 30%, there is always 30% sitting in the mystery period.

One way to look at turning informal into formal training is through some of the most common on-the-job learning activities. First, making joint calls or riding along with a veteran salesperson is standard practice in most sales organization. If done right, joint calls are very valuable. If done wrong, they are a waste of time.

Let's start by looking at the wrong way. Brett, the new salesperson, is sent out to ride along with Casey the old pro. There are no directions on what Brett should see or do. Should Brett see calls on current customers or just new prospects? Will Brett see initial presentations, closing calls, or something else?

Now, let's look at how to make this more deliberate and formal. The first step is to identify the types of calls Brett might see. These are typical:

- Calling to set appointments
- Initial presentation calls
- Presenting proposal calls
- Follow-up/service calls

If the organization is using a standard sales process or one of the hundreds of sales training programs, there are different names for these calls and maybe a few more. The idea is to map out the joint call strategy or process for these calls.

In a joint call for each of these types of calls, the new salesperson plays one of three roles. The first is as an observer. The salesperson is assigned to watch, take notes, and then discuss their observations after the call. As the salesperson progresses, the next role is to assist. This is a shared call with the salesperson taking more and more responsibility. The final role is the leader. The salesperson is taking charge with the manager there only to provide feedback after the call.

This sounds like a lot of calls, and it is. However, there isn't much learning in one or two ride alongs. Now there are tools to help turn these calls into learning opportunities. These tools are often derived from any formal sales training, if it exists. The tools include:

- Pre-call Plan
- Call checklist (1 for each type of call)
- Call debriefing form

By using this approach, it becomes more and more apparent how many joint calls are needed. It's more than one. It could be five or ten. It might be fifty. Once you know the number, you can put them on the Learning Path and make time and space for them. As you try to get the sequence right, you are mixing these calls with the product, technical and sales training.

It should be noted that it's often difficult to see meaningful calls that advance learning. Call centers have this issue. Instead of ride alongs, they have side by sides. I've listened to hundreds of calls in a call center, and the big problem is that you don't know what you are going to hear. Let's say I'm assigned to listen to order taking calls for three hours. In those three hours, 30 to 40 calls might come in, but they may have nothing to do with order taking. It might be someone calling in about a billing issue or asking to change an address or just asking to be transferred to another employee or even a wrong number or two. In a call center, it may be better to listen to selected recorded calls that are focused on the learning objective.

Now, let's look at manufacturing. In manufacturing, joint calls are replaced by job shadows and hands-on training. Let's start with something as straightforward as packaging. What helps is to have a standard way of doing hands-on training that can be applied to everything in the plant. There are a vast array of models. Use this model or pick one you like better. The key is to make it the standard.

1. Start with the Big Picture

    I have a friend who calls this getting the Gestalt. This comes from Gestalt psychology introduced in the 1890s. But for us, it simply means getting the big picture, seeing how everything works together before looking at all the steps. It's a fun word to say. So start by having the new operator watch the entire packaging process including looking at how the product got there and where it's going next. This sets the stage for learning.

2. Demo the steps

    Next, show how the packaging machine works while reinforcing all the safety requirements. If there is a standard work or SOP, have the new operator follow along. Do this a few times, but focus only on operations when the machine is working correctly.

3. Try it

    The new operator should then be given a chance to try it out. The trainer should be giving frequent feedback, and this trial should be repeated until the operator gets it right.

4. Practice

    The new operator now is going to practice with coaching. This might be a few hours or a few days. Getting enough repetitions is critical. The trainer is actively coaching initially and then backs off over time. Remember to track how many repetitions most new people need so you can make space for that activity on the Learning Path.

5. Troubleshoot

This is the time to deal with everything that goes wrong. Start with those problems that occur all the time and then work on the problems that are less frequent. Use the process of the demo, try it, and practice.

If the operation has multiple steps or multiple stations, look for the best sequence and go from simple to complex and easy to hard.

Insights from working in manufacturing can be applied to training in most other jobs. First, most modern manufacturing equipment works well and is easy to learn. The real training challenge involves what to do when something goes wrong. I've heard these so-called exceptions or upset conditions. The key is to make sure the employee is proficient in handling these problems.

Here's a quick and easy way to find these exceptions and build them into training. I start with the dreaded blank sheet of paper. I give it to the first operator and ask him/her to write two or three upset conditions or problems. I then tell him/her to pass it to another operator, lead, or manager and ask him/her to write two or three additional items and then pass it to the next person. After a quick trip around the plant, there is usually 30 to 50 items on the list. Then, I circulate the entire list and ask everyone to add anything we missed.

Now I ask the Learning Path team to divide this list into three buckets. Bucket 1 contains those issues that happen hourly or daily. Bucket 2 contains those problems that happen less frequently, maybe weekly or monthly. Bucket 3 contains those rare upset conditions that might be seen once a year. Initially, we are going to spend most of the time on Bucket 1. Toward the middle or end of the Learning Path we are going to take on Bucket 2. Bucket 3 items happen so rarely that usually only one or two people in the plant know what to do or have ever seen the problem. For a new person, all we teach is how to identify a problem and who to call for help.

The second big thing is about how to do practice. Practice is less about how much time is spent in practice and more about repetitions. I was working with a team of operators who mix batches of chemicals. I asked, "How many different batches are there?" They said, "It's about 10." Then I asked, "How many batches do you need to mix before you get good at it?" They said again, "It's about 10." So the practice on this Learning Path specified a practice time that included doing 10 repetitions of the 10 different batch types. This was much more productive than, say, practice mixing batches for the next three days.

Practice can sometimes be difficult to schedule. Sometimes, you can't get enough repetitions to get good at something. I worked with a job that required cutting with a welding torch. This is something they might do every week or two. This meant they were learning all over again each time. Learning to cut with a welding torch isn't that hard if you get enough practice. Now on their Learning Path, the employee is sent to the scrap pile with the welding torch to cut metal for three hours or until they become proficient. Practice sometimes requires setting up practice areas.

You can see that there are similarities between the sales and manufacturing areas. They both require a standardized teaching method, hours of practicing and coaching, specified numbers of repetitions and practice areas when it's difficult to get enough repetitions on the job.

I worked on a very interesting project that found a way to blend formal and informal together. Dakota Technical College had a grant to create a seven-week school for railroad conductors. The grant included three of the major rail companies.

The goal of the program was to prepare potential new conductors to be ready to go to work once they were hired. Most of this training involved safety and how not to get injured when working with rail cars. If you are looking the wrong way at the wrong time, a conductor can get hit by a train going the other way.

As part of the grant, the railroads donated eight freight cars and about five hundred feet of track. This was all set up outdoors so the students could work in the weather and time of day they would experience on the job.

The train was set up so that students would spend an hour or two in the classroom and then go out to their practice in a rail yard with the teacher to work with what they had learned first-hand. All of this was written down in a detailed manner so that there were directions for both the classroom and practice. As a result, each time the school was held, it covered the same material in the same way, including the informal time spent in the practice yard.

Managers as Trainers

Most informal learning that is not trial-and-error learning is done side by side with an expert, co-worker, manager, or supervisor. To maximize this type of learning, managers, and supervisors not only need to be involved, but they need to lead this process. I've read about this statement hundreds of times from other training leaders. Yet for some reason, in most organizations, it seldom happens. Managers and supervisors typically give the excuse that they are too busy, but there are other reasons for their reluctance.

Looking at job descriptions and performance appraisal documents, training employees isn't at the top of the list if it's there at all. Managers and supervisors are being compensated for production goals and other business measures, not training. So instead of having willing sign-ups to get involved with training, there are only volunteers. A Learning Path is a big change that can't be led from the grassroots.

An even bigger obstacle is that managers and supervisors don't know what to do and how to do it. What managers and supervisors need are:

- Training in how to do on-the-job training
- A recipe book that tells them in detail what to do and when to do it
- Job aides, checklists, and other training resources to help them out as they go along
- A Learning Path and proficiency definition that teaches them how to develop their people.

Without the involvement of managers and supervisors in training, they often manage at cross purposes to the training. You may have heard this statement, "That's great that you went through training, but let me show you what we do around here." This is why it's critical for managers and supervisors to be active participants on a Learning Path team for the functions they manage.

Other Informal Learning Opportunities

Making joint calls and learning hands-on are two of the most common and important informal learning activities. They become more formal and powerful by adding structure and finding ways to eliminate all the variability. There are several hundred other types of informal learning activities. If they are important, they should be done intentionally and not by accident.

In many jobs, it's a great idea to do networking both to make contacts and advance professionally. When I go to networking events such as association meetings, I see attendees talking with the people they already know. Most people are reluctant to get outside their comfort zone. It's like going to a class and sitting in the back row. You won't be noticed, and you can slip out easily. Networking is something that can and should be structured. It starts with a networking plan that might include numbers of contacts, follow-up activities, and active participation such as making presentations to the association.

This reminds me of going with my father to events held by the pharmaceutical companies. There was always a lecture by one of the researchers on a drug or therapy. At every meeting, two or three doctors who would ask all of the questions. My father would turn to me and remark, "That doctor already knows the answer to that question. He knows what he's talking about. He just wants to see if the presenter knows." However, in any of these events, some choose to actively participate while others are there for the dinner and entertainment.

Technology has made it possible to have robust online discussion groups, peer coaching, wikis, discussion boards, and more. Just putting them up and hoping that learners will get involved and get something out of them is usually a pipe dream. There has to be some type of direction and accountability.

I'm a fan of LinkedIn. They have hundreds or thousands of group. What you will see is that a group might have 25,000 members, but there are only a few discussions posted every week, usually by the same people. It takes work and effort to be involved. If it's part of an informal learning activity, don't expect it just to happen.

A Quick Way to Build Activities

It doesn't need to take a lot of time to turn informal learning into more formal learning activities. Here's what I do.

On any Learning Path, there may be thirty or more informal learning activities. I try to find an internal expert or experienced employee for each activity. I then go through a quick interview either in-person or on the phone.

The first thing I need to do is create a general overview of the activity. I ask, "What's this activity about" or "What's the purpose of this activity?" This is the "Gestalt." I'm just going to do an overview and not write learning objectives. As I've stated, learning objectives are usually overstated, and they don't have much value for non-trainers.

Let's say the activity is a job shadow with the marketing department. I'm asking questions so I can write this overview.

"This job shadow is about learning the roles and responsibilities of the marketing department and how they interact with other departments."

As part of this overview, I need to ask about how much time is needed for this activity, is it one hour, two hours or half a day?"

The next thing I do is just walk through the job. I ask, "What's the first thing you do?" "What's the next thing you do?" Usually, there are 5 or 6 steps. I also ask if there are any materials, documents, job aides, checklists, or anything else that is needed for this activity.

Then I circle back and ask if there is enough practice in this activity and what can be done for follow-up. It might be possible at this time to identify the number and type of practice repetitions.

This interview actually goes very fast. What I've done so far should take about 20 minutes. Now, I can go back and make sure everything fits into our model of doing informal training and put everything into the format we are going to use either in print or online.

Enhancing Learning Informal Learning Activities

In the last few years, Learning Paths have moved away from paper to online delivery. This makes it possible to link on-the-job training with a wide range of other training and support.

For example, before learning how to mix polymers, the operator can be linked to a short e-learning lesson or video. Adding links to standard work documents makes coaching easier. This makes learning activities more robust and interactive.

There is more and more technology that tracks and manages the interaction between coaches and employees. Capturing these interactions ensures that the activity actually happens and provides useful information for ongoing updates and enhancements to the Learning Path.

This chapter presented ways to take the mystery out of the "Mystery period." The bulk of all learning is going to be the informal, on-the-job training. It shouldn't be different for every learner, every time it's done. The key is to decide on methods and templates that can be used for every informal learning activity. It's like creating and writing down the recipe. This is going to make managers and supervisors better trainers because they don't need to decide what to do and how to do it for every new employee. They will have all of the tools and materials at their fingertips rather than having to dump out the drawers to find the missing manual to figure out what to do.

Finally, technology can make these activities more interactive and robust while making it easier to track and monitor these activities. Training is becoming more paperless.

CHAPTER 13:

Making It "Stick"

Is this the program of the month or the flavor of the day? Without paying a great deal of attention to implementation and maintenance, training initiatives will die on the vine.

Earlier I showed that the best way to build a Learning Path is to use a Learning Path team. Active participation is a critical change management technique for building buy-in and consensus.

I talked about not keeping the work of the Learning Path team secret and letting others know what the team is doing and why. In fact, the pool of those people involved expanded through all of the interviews.

Reviews

Another way you can expand the number of people involved is through reviews. Every part of the Learning Path needs to be reviewed and approved.

However, everyone doesn't need to review every part of the Learning Path. It's a lot to review. Assigning experts to review specific learning activities, cuts down the review time and work that's expected.

Nevertheless, as the project leader, you need to review everything with the help of someone who can do editing and proofing. If there are links to resources, someone has to check to make sure they work.

While brainstorming from a blank canvas is difficult for most people, reviewing documents is even less natural. I have been planning for a long time to do a little video that shows this dilemma. In the opening scene, we are looking at two characters on a veranda. Shakespeare is asking his good friend Francis Bacon to take a quick look at his new play and tell him what he thinks. Bacon scans through the manuscript turning pages and nodding frequently. Then he says, "I see here on page three that you misspelled melancholy."

That's not a good comment. Shakespeare wanted to know about the plot, the dialogue, and the settings. But left without directions, this is how most people do reviews.

Therefore, reviewers have to be given very specific directions about how to review and give comments. For example, tell reviewers to make sure that everything is technically correct. Also, look for anything that needs to be added or deleted.

Learning Path Library

Often a full Learning Path can have 50 to 100 learning activities. Most of these activities will connect to physical and digital resources. For example, any hands-on training in a manufacturing plant can relate directly to a standard work document, procedure manual, or SOP. Having quick and easy access to those documents makes the Learning Path come alive.

For salespeople, there can be sample sales presentations and proposals, product information, marketing literature, magazines, articles, and a wide array of websites and other online resources. There might be so much of this stuff that hunting it down when it's needed is near impossible. One easy technique to start gathering all of this material is to make it part of a scavenger hunt for new employees. As they visit departments and experts, they ask for and collect this information.

Some of the resources needed aren't print or digital based. A quality activity might include a pile of good and bad samples. There also might be videos and pictures.

With this in mind, it's crucial to assign a librarian. The librarian is responsible for building and maintaining a Learning Path Library. This might include creating an online, searchable database. In any case, the librarian is the only one that can add or remove items from the library. Another duty of the librarian is to maintain a current searchable catalog. Without this authority, the library is a free for all and loses its value quickly.

Launch

Imagine all of those old newsreels that showed the launch of a new ship where the champagne bottle doesn't break. Champagne bottles are designed to be hard to break, so steps are often taken to make sure the bottle breaks such as scoring the glass with a glass cutter. So having a successful launch requires preparation and thought.

There are key decisions to be made when launching a new Learning Path. Since this is process improvement, the new Learning Path is the next evolution of what's currently being done. It may have a big "wow" factor, but it's not designed to be perfect. A good launch plan should answer these questions:

- Are you going to do a pilot or roll it out all at once?
- How are you going to be training the mentors, coaches, and trainers?
- Is there a kickoff plan or meeting to inform that larger organization?
- How are you going to voice any top-level support for the Learning Path to the organization?
- How are you going to let those who worked on this initiative take full credit?

Keeper of the Path

The keeper of the path is similar to the librarian. The keeper of the path is charged with maintaining the integrity of the Learning Path and all of the activities. The keeper of the path is the only one who can make changes to the Learning Path and any related documents.

If anyone can make changes at any time, it's unlikely that everyone will be using or on the same path. The keeper is even more critical in environments where procedures change almost daily such as in a call center.

Tinkering

With any process, there is always the hazard of doing too much tinkering. Constantly making small adjustments and changes can drive too much waste and variability into the system. Each new person shouldn't be going through a Learning Path that was modified since the last trainee.

In fact, there's a trap of changing the Learning Path before it's been fully tested. Instead, the best approach is to schedule update or improvement meetings once or twice a year looking at all possible changes at once. There should be new ideas and time to do a second or third round of upgrades. Changes to the path are different from changes to the supporting documents. Those documents need to be changed to fit the current business situation. If you are linking documents, the changes can be made without changing the link.

This chapter presented some ideas on how to implement, launch, and maintain a Learning Path. It requires support and consensus from all the key players to make it work. If you have a strong project champion and an active Learning Path team, you are well on your way to making it stick.

CHAPTER 14:

More for Less

Throughout this book, I've talked about how eliminating waste and variability reduces time and cost. Certainly, reducing the amount of retraining required makes good financial sense. With that theme in mind, I'd like to present some ideas for those who lead learning organizations or training departments to maximize budgets and reduce costs without sacrificing results.

Reducing Variability

Let's look at variability. So, as you look across the organization and all the training that gets done, think about what can be standardized or made consistent. The chapter on learning principles presented the starting point. If everything fits your learning principles, training will become more consistent. This means that when you use vendors, they need to follow your principles and not the other way around.

The next place to look is at all the decisions that are made on training initiatives and considered which of these decisions can be made in advance and then applied to all training initiatives.

Cost Effectiveness

I think one of the more interesting decisions is to determine the best use of each type of learning method which includes, classroom training, e-learning, on-the-job training, web conferences, social learning, and simulations. There are more, but these are the basic types. Classroom training is good for some training and not as good for others. The same with e-learning—it is not a panacea for all training.

I've found that classroom training does an excellent job on anything that requires interaction and discussion among participants. For example, something like practicing presentations is better in front of a live audience. Role-playing works better in person than on a web conference.

Classrooms are not as good for heavy delivery of content. Because of time constraints too much gets loaded into a short period of time. As a result, a lot of it's forgotten and has to be done again later. Moving content to self-study or something like e-learning tends to work better.

Other limitations might make one form of training better than another. For example, training large audiences that are geographically dispersed is a logistical nightmare and very costly. On the other hand, building e-learning for a 5-person audience with content that needs to be delivered quickly and won't be repeated is a waste of time.

To avoid having to do this type of analysis every time a training program needs to be built is unnecessary and an expensive waste of time. Do it once and set out the rules or guidelines. You can even create a slide presentation that explains your position for each and every training program. It helps you make better buying decisions when you buy services and training from the outside.

Systems, Processes, and Templates

Another place to look for cost savings involves all of the processes of designing and delivering training. The process of researching, designing, building, and delivering training can be done in a thousand different ways. One good one is all you need.

ADDIE and AGILE are two of the most popular design models for training. There are pluses and minuses to each, and it's not important to discuss it here. My point is that picking one and then using it for everything is better than deciding every time. Maybe you want to create a hybrid or your own model? That's great as long as it's detailed out and all the tools and templates are there. If you are going to make a change, then everyone has to change with you.

Standardizing tools and templates are the next big thing. Here are just a few items that can be standardized and then supported:

- Needs Assessment
- Proposals
- Design Documents
- Workshop Materials
- E-learning Templates
- Results Reports

To show you the value of a template, about fifteen years ago, I put a small little post on a training discussion board offering a standard format for a facilitator guide. I hadn't imagined that from one post that I would get over a thousand requests. I don't know why but I still get a few requests. But it was this need for standardization that was driving this need.

Let's talk waste. Eliminating anything that doesn't add value is the fastest way to save money. There is an activity I call dumping out the drawers which eliminates building training when something already exists. This is a quick process of uncovering everything that relates to training concerning a specific job or task. This could be manuals, job aides, videos, pictures, slide presentations, or even course catalogs. Almost no one in the organization knows what exists and where it can be found.

I was working with a large healthcare company, and they wanted to add some financial training for their administrators. They were about to embark on building this course when someone in human resources said that they had done something similar to that five years ago and thought the team had gone through it. It turns out the program was in a desk in human resources, and no one had ever seen it. It turned out to be exactly what they were looking for.

The bigger the organization, the more this situation exists. On the flip side, you might find that there is a training going on that shouldn't be. Taking the ax to this type of training is the fastest way to cut costs without spending any money.

The Learning Paths methodology does provide an easy pathway to looking at both variability and waste. It works in every other part of an organization, so why not training. Learning Paths standardizes how to approach any situation where training is required. Having a proven process is much better than trying to think one up each time.

Training Delivery

A final consideration is how the training is going to be delivered. For example, I changed how I did workshops about ten years ago. Participants wanted me to stop killing trees. So I got rid of 100-page participant guides. I found that no one looked at his or her participant guide after the training. The first step was to redesign classroom training so that participants would bring in something to work on during the class. Salespeople would bring in information about a current client or two, Learning Path project leaders would bring in a job assigned to them, and managers might bring in a key problem or issue.

Second, I would ask everyone to bring their laptops to class with all the information they would need. There would be a prework assignment on how to gather this information. Third, the workshop would focus on working on real situations, and all the classroom materials would be delivered online or through a flash drive. Instead of taking notes by hand, they would write directly into the documents on their computers. Some of the output of the class would be already in templates which would give them a jump start on what they would do next. I used to offer participants a hard copy of the materials, and almost everyone left them on the tables at the end of the class.

Today, all of the Learning Path outputs from proficiency definitions through learning activities are delivered either online or are paper-based. There are some manufacturing environments where you can't bring smartphones, laptops, and tablets into the plant. Paper is still the best option. For others, the online version is a big advantage. First, there is a documentation trail for every activity including assessments. Any activity can easily be linked to a database of procedures, instruction manuals, videos, e-learning, and job aides. Everything is there as you need it.

Second, everything is easier to update and keep current. In some companies, procedures can change every day. Third, paper tends to get lost. Online training is always there and always available. Finally, some of the new technology allows an expanded ability to do online coaching and manage the interaction between learning and coaching. This is a rapidly expanding opportunity that offers a lot of promise.

An online, complete Learning Path offers an additional and somewhat unexpected benefit. Imagine two companies. The first does very traditional training. A new candidate, probably a millennial, asks the question, what's going to be my training. The interviewer can pull out a huge binder or show a course catalog. This is interesting but not overly impressive. The second company has a robust online Learning Path. The candidate can see on a tablet that everything is there and that there is a detailed plan for improvement. This becomes a big competitive advantage when going after top recruits. I heard about this first from an insurance client who was going after graduates of top business schools.

This chapter focused on how to save money and be more efficient by decided what to do in advance and putting in systems and processes to make it work. Every project doesn't need to be new and different all the time. The end result is that training will be more consistent and yield better results.

CHAPTER 15:

The Sales Learning Path

I originally learned about sales training in the mid-70s from a friend's father-in-law who had been one of Dale Carnegie's original top salespeople. Sales training back in the early 50s was designed to help all the veterans coming back from World War II, succeed in door-to-door selling. Since then I've run into just about every sales model you can imagine. It's hard to keep track of them all because there were so many.

The World of Sales Training

I did work for some time customizing Wilson Learning's Counselor selling which was big in the era of consultative selling a concept made popular by Mack Hanan. I remember the fascination people had with SPIN Selling and Miller Heiman's Strategic Selling. I have seen many of the sales training programs built on the foundation of PSS1 and 2. (This has its roots in Xerox Selling Systems.) I haven't read all the sales training books. Amazon lists over 12,000 sales training books with over 200 relating to consultative selling alone.

All of these programs have their pluses and minuses, but they do provide a common approach and sales language which makes sales training much easier and effective. So, in this chapter, I don't want to compete with these programs. Instead, I want to examine how to develop salespeople using Learning Paths.

Let's talk for a minute about what's missing in most sales training. Consider that you've just taken the world's best five-day sales training program. The following Monday when you go back to work, are you now the top-selling salesperson? Probably not.

For one thing, you've never tried out all the new sales training on a real customer. Talking with real customers is very different from role-plays or simulations. The customer doesn't have a script, and even if they did, they have no incentive to stick with the script.

This reminds me of a time that I was working on a customer service training program for hotel reservations. An associate came up with a superior training video that explained the challenges of customer service training. In the opening scene, a customer was standing in line behind two other people checking in. He kept trying to get the front desk clerks attention while explaining that he was in a hurry. In the next scene, the front desk clerk takes the guest aside and explains that because the guest was rude, he would have to go through customer training before being allowed to check in. In the final scene, the guest was in customer training class learning the 5 rules of being a good customer. I remember that rule 5 was tip big and tip often.

The point of the video was that we have to train the front desk in customer service because we can't train the customer. In fact, there will be some concepts in customer service training that will be a real challenge with real customers. The same thing is true with all of the sales skill training. A good closing question doesn't work well on a customer who wasn't paying attention.

Beyond Formal Sales Training

What's missing in most sales training is everything that is specific to a particular sales job. Consider what's missing between a top real estate agent and a top chemical engineering salesperson. Other than the product, the technology, the market, the customers, the type of sale, and company differences, these two sales jobs are identical. That's far more than a sales process or selling skills.

I've been working with travel agents since the mid-90s, thousands of them. I am very good now at helping others with their vacation plans. Travel provides a good example of the differences in sales jobs and how there isn't a single Learning Path for all travel agent jobs. There are four entirely different travel agent's jobs with a big split between leisure and business agents. Leisure agents are focused on building great vacations and trips for their customers. Upgrading to a better cruise cabin or adding on a rafting trip are the types of things leisure agents add-on at an additional cost to try to delight the customer.

On the other hand, business travel is all about cost control and enforcing travel policy. The choice between which airline or hotel to offer is based first on where the company has negotiated the best rates. A business agent will often say, you have to fly economy with one stop in Atlanta. A leisure agent will only say this if it's the only option that fits what the customer wants.

In reality, some agents will sell leisure travel while others will only sell business travel. Within leisure travel, you have agents working in large call centers in a highly transactional sales process. They aren't concerned with building a clientele. Travel agents who work in agencies, on the other hand, only succeed long term by building a loyal clientele of customers who travel several times per year.

The major differences in the Learning Paths for these two agents are that a travel agent in an agency needs more training on how to find and keep customers. They will get more involved with marketing and even social media. One type of agent is answering the phone while the other is trying to make the phone ring.

The two types of business travel agents have night and day differences. The first type of agent is handling calls to book travel. Their Learning Path involves processing transactions quickly without error and dealing with customers including enforcing travel policy. They are operating under very strict guidelines. The other type of business agent sells travel management services to clients which is a typical business-to-business sales process. The agent goes out to a company and says, "We want to handle all your travel." They don't need to know about exotic destinations or resorts. Instead, they need to know the ins and outs of managing travel. More than anything, this is a financial sale to someone like a CFO who wants to set budgets and monitor costs.

There is a third type of business agent. This agent is involved in meeting planning. For the most part, their customers are meeting and event planners. For leisure travel, this means events like destination weddings and family reunions. This type of selling weighs heavily on getting all the details right and dealing with different suppliers.

As you can see, even though these are all travel agents, their jobs, and type of selling is very different. An agent booking a resort for a family of four at Disney World is very different from the agent convincing a local school system to book their travel through their agencies.

Each Learning Path has some common core elements; they diverge quickly from the sales process, product, and technology. In looking at proficiency definitions, each of these jobs is measured differently. An agent is a call center might be measured on calls per hour, talk time, average room rate, and overall sales. An agent calling on business might be measured by the number of new customers, fees from existing customers, and numbers of referrals.

Unique Sales Positions

The point of all this is that the proficiency definitions and Learning Paths for each sales position are unique. While sales training programs can be a part of the path, they are only a small part of the path. However, there is a large challenge in getting sales training to transfer to the job. Traditionally, there is a tendency to teach everything separately and then hope it all comes together.

A good example of this comes from working with business insurance salespeople. These salespeople have to know a wide range of coverages inside and out. However, just knowing about commercial liability insurance doesn't mean you can sell it. In selling commercial liability, salespeople have to find out who are the potential customers, where the biggest opportunities lie, how to connect this coverage to individual customers, how to propose and price this coverage, and how to get renewals. Along the way, they will have to learn to work with underwriters and insurance companies. A good Learning Path has to blend all of these factors together.

Finally, this brings us to yet one more type of selling that is completely different from the other ones so far. That's the type of selling where the salesperson doesn't actually sign a contract or make a sale. This is more common than you think. Here are two examples, in which the selling is similar, but the Learning Path is very different.

First is pharmaceutical sales. The financial transaction for pharmaceutical sales occurs between a pharmacy and a drug company or a pharmacy and a consumer. The physician selects the drugs and can be influenced by the pharmaceutical rep. Instead of making sales presentations, the rep details the drug and answers questions. The challenge of pharmaceutical sales is to get access and build relationships with doctors. The rep is compensated in part by sales of a particular drug from an entire territory. The Learning Path for a pharmaceutical rep is highly focused on detailing drugs and building relationships with doctors. The rep doesn't need to know minor option closes in this training because closing the sale isn't part of this sales process.

Second, let's look at industrial sales involving raw materials such as polymers, chemicals, or metals. These companies are the bottom or start of the supply chain. What they make is sold to companies who blend raw materials or make parts or subassemblies. All the contracts are signed at the lower levels of the supply chain. However, influencing these sales happens further up the supply chain.

At the top of the chain might be an airline company. Airline manufacturers don't buy rubber for airplane wheels. What they buy are complete wheel assemblies to be put on the planes. Tires are just one part of the wheel assembly, but it's the tire manufacturers who will buy the rubber. However, at the airplane manufacturer, they might specify the performance they want out of their tires. This means a different formula for the tires might be needed.

For this type of salesperson, the job becomes building relationships at the airplane company so that their engineers become part of creating the specs for tires and rubber. Not only isn't there a contract to sign, but these sales can be long term. If it takes 5 to 10 years to launch a new airplane, it might be 3 or 4 years before anyone thinks about the tires.

In sales training, experts often talk about a top-down or bottom-up selling. This type of selling is more side to side because of all of the internal departments that will affect the final product. Contacts have to be made in engineering, safety, quality, marketing, and more. The president of this company isn't going to have a great interest in the composition of the rubber in the tires, but all these departments might.

As you can see, there is quite a range of sales positions. Some take a few months to learn while others take years. Blending all the sales training with the product training while adding all the practice, coaching, and experience have to be combined into a Learning Path to reduce time to proficiency.

I want to put in a final word for designing sales training to get quick results while improving the transfer of skills and knowledge to the job. I've done this may be two dozen times, and it always seems to work. This is typically an approach for business-to-business selling.

The training might be involved with installing a sales process or building sales skills. For prework, I give the assignment to profile either a new or an existing customer that the salesperson wants to work with. I have people bring in their laptops because they will be doing real work in the session. During the session, I teach a concept or approach with perhaps a template such as a prospecting plan. Then there is time to apply that to the account the salesperson brought to class. At the end of the class, the salesperson has a clear plan on what to do next and how to do it.

The sales manager is then given a follow-up plan as a way to evaluate the salesperson performance against what's been taught. After they've had a chance to work on their strategy, they might present their results to the other participants in the class. In these presentations, it's surprising on how much has been sold and how much larger the sales were than expected. I find that success is an important glue to making things stick.

This chapter has examined different types of sales positions and their potential Learning Paths. The big point is that sales training isn't a one size fits all and that sales skills are just a small part of the picture. In addition, all the pieces and parts of learning to sell have to be put together because that's how they are used.

CHAPTER 16:

The Path to Leadership

Amazon has over 187,000 books on leadership. Some examine great leaders, and others talk about the qualities of a leader. As a result, this chapter is not about either. Instead, this chapter is going to examine "how" to develop leaders by applying the principles and concepts of Learning Paths. I don't think anyone enters a three-day leadership workshop and then exits as a great leader. There's more to it, and it might take years.

Where to Start

Part of the dilemma is that there are so many different positions of leadership and real-life situations, that a one size fits all solutions doesn't work. Leading a small project team is very different from leading a large organization with 100,000 employees. Some leadership positions come with a great amount of power and authority while others have none at all. Going from one to another isn't all that easy.

Imagine that you are going to lead a project team of scientists even though you barely got through high school physics. Even with great leadership qualities, you're going to have a tough time when the team asks your opinion on the strings to mathematical equations on their whiteboard. All they need to know from you is whether or not they are on the right track.

Now imagine you are the CEO of a major corporation, but you don't know much about financial statements. In this case, there is a strong case to be made that you will lead this company off a financial cliff. While great leaders have a great team around them, it's hard to motivate others when you don't speak the same language especially if the language is math or science.

Just as we discussed in the last chapter that selling is more than just sales skills, leadership is much more than just leadership skills. Leadership is something you can't master in a three-day workshop because like everything else it takes practice, coaching, and experience.

As leaders move up in an organization, they can easily lose touch with how work is done. They can't address all the issues they don't see or understand. The "Just get it done" leader often fails because of being out of touch with the capabilities of the organization, just how long it takes and what it's going to cost. It's a little like yelling at a cake to bake faster.

What Do Leaders Produce

From the starting point of leadership training, the Learning Path's approach is to ask the question, "What do leaders produce?" There are some general results or outcomes that all leader's produce such as timely and effective decisions or a highly motivated team that gets things done. However, the issue is much more specific when it relates to a leadership position. A project leader might produce solutions to technical problems that are on time and within budget. On the other hand, a senior leader might produce a higher return for shareholders.

As with every position, there can be a proficiency definition of 30 to 60 statements that describe output, quality, time, and safety. I put in safety because one output might be creating a safe environment or culture, or where accidents are below a given level.

One of the more popular parts of leadership is creating a vision. A proficiency statement would describe the desired result of that vision, (in order to do what?). On the other hand, not every leadership position should be creating visions. An organization doesn't need 50 or 100 visions. Most leaders are implementing the organization's vision.

Often the difference between a manager and a leader is blurred. They do many of the same work. Frequently a good manager needs to be a good leader, and a good leader needs to be a manager. When building a proficiency definition or Learning Path for a certain role, it's not that critical to divide the two. In fact, it's not a bad idea to include both.

A Learning Path for Leaders

Let's talk about a Learning Path for leadership. In most cases, it looks similar to a career path with the emerging leader going from one type of project to the next as well as from one leadership position to the next. Consider the following when building a leadership Learning Path for a project leader. Ask these questions:

- What types of projects will be led?
- How many projects need to be led to become proficient?
- What formal and informal training needs to be planned along the way?

As we talked about already, the starting point is not to invent a leadership curriculum. Start by finding the current path by asking, how do project leaders become proficient today? Then map it out. Once it's mapped do the following:

- Compare it to the proficiency definition. What can be added or deleted?

- Find an organizing principle and structure the path in the most effective manner
- Make the informal activities such as participating on a project, formal or structured
- Put in place reviews at key milestones

In many cases, organizations hire leaders with a great deal of previous experience either at the same or a slightly lower level. A custom Learning Path is created by eliminating those items from the Learning Path that has already been completed.

Setting this discussion aside, there are a lot of mythologies and even research that surrounds the issue of leadership. In many ways, we are teaching leaders how we would like them to be rather than how they are. There is a big difference between being an effective leader and a good person. An effective leader gets results with and through other people. Think about two different football coaches. The first yells and screams at the player while demanding a lot out of them. The second coach is more soft-spoken and tries to find a way to motivate players. Both coaches win a Super Bowl, so both coaches are effective.

Being a good person has more to do with how the leader treats and motivates people. This might be something the organization desires, but it's not the only way to be effective. So it's important when creating a proficiency definition to describe what your organization wants fully.

A great deal of leadership revolves around how to motivate others. There are as many studies on motivation as there are on leadership. I am always somewhat cautious about the conclusions of these studies because of flaws in the methodology.

I am sure that you've heard that money isn't the most important motivator for people. Something like praise from the boss or fitting in with coworkers is always higher. These aren't quantified answers. Is money a big motivator? Well, how much money are we talking about? A dollar, fifty thousand dollars? Or five million dollars aren't the same.

How about praise from the boss? Does this mean when you do well? Every day no matter what or every ten minutes. It's a certain amount of recognition and when it's given that makes a difference. Would you prefer praise every ten minutes or five million dollars?

This reminds me of a story from my early days in training. It was one of the first projects I ever did. I was working on designing a series of programs on motivation using the Plato System. The Plato System was part of the old Control Data and was the forerunner to computer-based training. I was assigned to create a simulation game to teach motivation. This was state of the art that all the graphics were stick figures. Since I was new, I was told that two things make a successful computer game—"competition and death."

The point of this discussion is to say that if it's important what you want a leader to do and how you want them to do it, you need to put that in your proficiency definition and have a series of learning activities that make it happen.

The question of who should be the leader is most often made at an executive level. Training's role is to develop the people top management designates. So it's important to know what you are starting with. However, a common discussion is where the leader should be a top performer. Some people say it's and some people say it's not. There is an argument for both but not a clear answer.

In sports, some great players have been great coaches, and yet many have not. There are as many examples of each. John Wooden, the legendary basketball coach at UCLA, had a record 12 NCAA championships including 7 in a row. What most people don't know is that he was the top college basketball player in the country for 2 years at Purdue. Ted Williams who was the last man to bat .400 for the Boston Red Socks has a career coaching record of 273 wins and 429 losses.

There are enough examples of both to say that there isn't a direct connection between being a great player and a great coach, but it should never be a disqualifier. There are some real benefits to using top performers as leaders. The most important is that they have knowledge and experience that only comes from performing in critical situations.

I was in Phoenix about ten year ago hitting golf balls on a range next to a player on the senior tour. He told me to be careful where I got instructions. There are secrets that tour players learned that a typical club pro would never have been exposed to. In the military, what you learn from being under fire you would never learn in any other way.

On the other hand, there are some drawbacks. These top performers haven't been in a leadership position, so it's all new to them. Many haven't done an analysis of the game or what they do because much of it comes naturally to them. They not only need to know how to do things but also how to explain them. There are some very good coaches who frequently took notes while they sat on the bench.

Are leaders born or can you develop them? It's hard to say. However, in today's more technical workplace, leaders will need to be able to speak the language of tech and see the vision of tech in the future. I don't think Luddites will make good leaders.

When designating new leaders, the Learning Paths approach can be used to make more informed decisions. The proficiency definition and Learning Path provide valuable information about the true nature of the position and what it will take to develop a new leader fully.

CHAPTER 17:

Learning Paths in Schools

I've often said that one of the foundational concepts behind Learning Paths came from a short video by Don Novello in his character of Father Guido Sarducci (you may have seen him on *Saturday Night Live*). It's one of those things that is funny because it's true. The video is called, "the five-minute university." The idea is that in five minutes, you learn what the average college graduate remembers 2 years after he or she is out of college. This video is still on YouTube, and I highly recommend it.

The video is one of the best illustrations of waste in learning. What you don't remember has absolutely no value; so either it needs to be taught differently or not at all. To illustrate this point, when I'm doing speeches I ask, "How many people took a foreign language in school?" Most people raise their hands. I ask, "How many people took Spanish?" About half the hands in the room go up. Then I say, "Imagine two years after you graduated, we flew you down to Mexico City, and of course, you would be speaking Spanish like a native?" I hear almost everyone laugh. Everyone knows that even with the best of education, after two years they are not going to remember much or be able to use what they've learned.

I took three languages in school, Latin, French, and Hebrew. It was one of the most confusing times of my life. I was always mixing up my vocabulary between languages. None of the time in Latin class was spent on speaking Latin because no one speaks Latin. Instead, we translated classics like Homer and Julius Caesar. I do remember that Gaul was divided into three parts but not much more. In French class, there was some work on speaking French but more time spent on reading French literature. In those days, the Theater of the Absurd was big. This was something that didn't make sense in English, so it didn't get any better in French.

Anyone who has ever been to Hebrew school will tell you that most of your time is spent preparing for your bar mitzvah. The goal was to teach you how to read Hebrew even if you didn't know what the words mean. Today, I still have a twenty-five-word Hebrew vocabulary, about half of what I remember from French. As a comparison, my little dog Sasha has about a 25-word vocabulary.

Foreign languages are just like learning anything else. Unless you spend hours and hours practicing including in real-life situations, you never get good at it, and it never sticks. I remember trying to speak French when I was in Paris after college. They looked at me like I was from another planet and pretended they couldn't hear me. By then it was too late to get a refund from my French teacher.

It's been a long time since I've been in school and I know there have been changes. However, when I was in high school, I sat in a study hall desk that my mother sat in during the 1940s and my uncle sat in during the 1930s. The big difference in our educations was that there were twenty or thirty more years of history to study, and I was the recipient of new math. New math was the concept that it wasn't the answer that was important but how you got there. There were also more initials carved into the desks.

Earlier I spent five years in a private school through ninth grade because my parents were trying to avoid sending us to a public junior high school. To get into this school, I had to take an entrance test. I failed the math test because I was a year behind coming out of a public school. This was one of the best public grade schools in Minneapolis. So, with the help of a tutor, I jumped a year and a half in math in order to start in the fall without being put back a grade. In contrast, wife Pamela skipped third grade and unfortunately missed most of the jokes kids tell.

The pace of learning at this private school was considerably faster. When I went back to go to a public high school, I felt that I didn't need to do much studying because I'd already covered this material. This continued into college. I remember getting a reading list in a humanities course in my sophomore year. Three of the books listed, I had read in ninth grade. One of them I had read in Latin.

I only relate these experiences to reveal any biases I might have going into a discussion about schools. However, the fact that everyone's experience is different and every school and every class are different illustrates a massive amount of variability which affects the quality of education.

The Learning Paths School

In this chapter, I'm going to try to set aside a critique of how schools operate. Schools have a long history and an extensive infrastructure. Public and private schools don't change easily, but they are really good at figuring out why new ideas won't work. Instead, what I want to do is wipe the slate clean and have you imagine what a Learning Paths school would look like. Since it's in our imagination, we can do anything we want including spending money.

As the architects of our new school, we are going to start by replacing graduation day with proficiency day. This is the day individual students reach 100% proficiency. We are going to replace grades and grade levels with proficiency milestones. Instead of being done at a set time, we will be done when we are done.

For those who got an education degree, one of the few theories you might have remembered is Benjamin Bloom's theory of mastery learning. It's the idea that student must reach the level of performance before moving on. The concept of mastery learning has great merit, but it does require schools to change completely.

The big difference in a Learning Paths school is how we look at levels of performance and the overall desired results. We don't want you to master algebra and never use it again after graduation. We also don't want you to learn to read and then never pick up a book after college.

The starting point for our Learning Paths school is to determine what we want students to be able to do after graduation. The idea is to push it at least one more level so that there is a practical result or outcome. Take the objective; students will be able to solve algebraic equations. Then ask the question, "in order to do what? Take another objective; students will know how each branch of government works. Then ask, "so that what?" Asking that question once might still be at too low a level so you might want to ask it several times.

Lifelong Learners?

Let's explore the concept of lifelong learners. While that's a lofty goal, you still can ask, "in order to do what?" It could be something that would include being able to solve problems as they happen or being able to prepare for new opportunities and challenges. However, how you define lifelong learning is going to shape how it's taught. It's not going to be something that is taught in one course or even in one year. It starts to break down traditional discipline and how education is grouped. You might not take history and English separately; you might take parts of them together.

For lifelong learners, reading is probably very important. The first thing we want to do is set a reading level that enables being a great lifelong learner. I think you will find that lifelong learners are reading all the time. We aren't going to learn to read at grade level. Instead, we are going to read at a level that brings in volumes of information every day. The average person reads about 300 words per minute while the average college student reads about 450 words per minute. The average speed reader reads 1500 word per minute. This gives us a good idea of where we might want to set our reading level. We know that when we go beyond about 500 words per minute, it means we have to change how we are teaching reading.

For the sake of argument, let's say that our graduates will read at 650 words per minute with 90% comprehension. We are going to start on this on day one and continue until this level is reached. It's different from teaching reading fundamentals and then hoping that the student gets better over time. We are going to have structured coaching and practice that may take years, but the outcome is worth it.

Here's the big side benefit. Reading at 650 words per minute, you could finish a 200-page book in less than 90 minutes. If you read for 90 minutes every day, in a typical school year you would read about 250 books. In twelve years, you would read 3,000 books. Reading 3000 books about anything makes a huge difference in anyone's education. However, at the Learning Paths school, we can guide the student through a selection of books to help meet other proficiencies. It doesn't have to be books. Reading at this speed allows you to read a 1000-word article every two minutes. You could easily get through 30 full articles in a day. What we are doing here is building a discipline. We are building reading as a habit through years of practice.

What amazes me is that someone can go through 12 years of school and not be able to read. I'm talking about someone who doesn't have a learning disability. It's very simple to determine if someone can read and then decide on what to do next. You hand them a book and ask them to read it to you. If you are working on reading every day, this issue gets addressed quickly.

Major Changes

I am not going to show a complete curriculum for a Learning Path style school but instead, show you some ideas and opportunities for change. I have often thought about what I could have learned earlier that would have helped me in the business world. One of those skills is meeting and interacting with people you don't know. Earlier I described how people go to networking events and spend all their time with people they already know. If they have become good at networking, they've done it on their own.

In a school environment, you get dumped together with other students exactly your same age. The instructions are, behave yourself, and we hope everything works out. What you end up with are some students who know everyone and are well liked, and others who won't talk to anyone. Some are comfortable in this situation, and others are terrified. Some say high school was the best time of my life while others say it was a nightmare.

What if there was a proficiency statement concerning meeting and interacting with others in the classroom and social situations. Not just behaving properly, but getting something out of the interaction, I think that would be very valuable and transfer to life after school. Again, this is not a single class but a combination of formal learning, practice, and experience that continues over many years. It might need to include others outside the school and a wider range of people.

I've heard about the need to teach critical thinking. This is another important, ill-defined concept. Here is an interesting way to look at critical thinking for our Learning Paths school. The last two books I read were about the Talpiot. This is one of the most elite groups in the Israeli Defense Force (IDF) and masters of teaching thinking. The Talpiot recruits extreme, highly intelligent high school students. These are not your typical nerds who skip out of gym class. They have to be able to complete the training for any of the units in the IDF.

The basic training for Talpiot is to get two college degrees in a discipline such as chemistry, physics, biology, or computer science. This has to be done in three years or less. During this time, they are going through basic training and rotations with different military groups such as the tank core or paratroopers. As they go through their training, they start working on what will be their ultimate goal. Their goal is to find technical solutions to real-life problems quickly. Instead of being taught just critical thinking, they are taught how to think in a way that nothing is impossible. The blending of real-life situations that are often under pressure with formal training helps them excel in unbelievable ways.

So going full circle back to our goal of teaching critical thinking, we have to think about what formal training is available but what experiences and practices are going to make a difference. You don't become a critical thinker overnight. We want to examine what it means to be a critical thinker. We might want them to be innovative and creative thinkers.

As you can see, this is not breaking down into the traditional curriculum of history, math, chemistry, English, and Spanish. These are probably going to be part of something larger or combined together. It can be hard or impossible to get agreement on these larger proficiency statements, but when there is agreement, it opens up a faster and more useful approach.

As we build this new curriculum, I'd like to put in a word for best practices. Today, there are about 36,000 high schools both public and private. Most schools have at least two tenth grade history classes on any given day. That means there are 72,000 different ways history is being taught. As a result, some are good, more are okay, and some are very poor, a natural result of high variability does. It's rare that you are in the classroom with the best history teacher. The question becomes what can we do to share the best of the best instead of taking potluck. I know I get more out of one hour watching the history channel that I did in a semester of high school. Of course, we are going to learn a lot about history reading our 200 books each year.

As we build the Learning Paths school, we should reexamine the role of teachers. I think that one of the reasons we have a teacher standing up in front of twenty or thirty students is because that's the way it's always been. There are lots of education practices that are done because that's the way it's always been done. Why do we have k-12—bottom line is because it's always been done that way. Originally when everyone worked on farms, there was a reason for 3 months off in the summer. But now, it's just habit.

I think the best role for teachers is to provide the tutoring, coaching, and mentoring students need. They would have more time to do this if they didn't have to create lesson plans, prepare lectures, or decide what to do every day. That could be done by our best practice experts who could do this for multiple schools at the same time. Again, this isn't a perfect solution, but it's moving in the right directions.

No discussion of schools can be complete without talking about testing. The only test of real value would be whether or not students are becoming proficient at the proficiency milestones. This isn't done through standardized multiple choice tests but rather through direct observation by teachers using the proficiency definitions and checklists. While this will take more time, it has a great deal of value instead of testing the student's ability to memorize enough to pass a test.

Here's an example. One of my friends in China relayed how his daughter had been evaluated in her art class. Instead of creating art and then having it reviewed by a teacher, she actually created an art piece while being observed by a panel of art teachers. They wanted to see both the art she created and the process that she used to create it. This is a much more in-depth and useful evaluation.

A final note on where some of the money comes from to do this type of change. Today, those who graduate typically do so sometime in June on their last day. Although they all learn at different rates and may have taken different courses, they all get there together. What would change if students just finished when they were proficient? There would be many students finishing in 9 years, 10 years, and 11 years. This would reduce the cost of teachers, facilities, and administration. This money could then be spent on providing more resources for students. I haven't done the math on this, but I guess that it's significant.

CHAPTER 18:

Getting It Together: Mergers, Acquisitions, Outsourcing, and Centralization

Mergers, acquisitions, outsourcing, and centralization have a common thread that a Learning Paths initiative can address. In each of these situations, multiple ways of doing a job need to be reduced to a single best practice approach. Also, there will be new jobs that are a combination of jobs, and some jobs will be split into multiple jobs. In any case, there is usually little or no consensus or feuding from one faction to another. Because there are only jobs descriptions and not proficiency definitions, these jobs are often ill-defined.

Mergers and Acquisitions

Companies merge or acquire on another because they feel that the combination of companies increases value or makes them more competitive. Mergers and acquisitions (M&A) often attempt to merge cultures and people in a way that just isn't going to work. My friend Ed Robbins who has worked in M&A for more than 30 years reminds me that most mergers and acquisitions fail and usually for the same reasons.

From a training perspective, a key issue is that a lot of the talent is on the way out the door or shopping their resumes. This happens because they feel uncomfortable, uncertain, or unappreciated. As they leave, they are talking a great deal of the companies knowledge and skill with them. The merged company is starting from scratch.

In this case, a Learning Path can be created to transition these employees into the new organization and their new roles. If done correctly, this can greatly reduce the flight of talent.

Successful mergers and acquisition use highly effect integration teams. These teams look at systems and processes as well as culture and leadership. They would be even more effective if they used a Learning Path team to work on the training issues for each job. As I talked about in the technology chapter

Training Priorities

When making a major organizational change, training is usually the last thought. I can't tell you how many times I've seen it when companies spend years planning a change and then start thinking about training in the last few weeks. Here's an extreme example. I was asked to build training for a company that was centralizing several back-office functions into a service center. Some of the staff were being relocated to the center, but most were brand new. I was asked to do this on Monday because the center was going to open on Thursday.

It took a long while for the center to become productive. The strategy for building training almost overnight was to involve the new employees in gathering all of the information they were going to need from the various internal experts. This scavenger hunt approach creates an interesting learning experience.

A good starting point for this discussion is to examine how to move or replicate a job from one location to another. I am one of the few people who has worked on moving a call center from India to Poland. The staff in India found it difficult to service Europe because they didn't have the language skills for German and French.

The call center in India had completed a Learning Paths project that included a proficiency definition, Learning Path and supporting training. It was a complete recipe for getting new employees proficient in a very short period of time. This is critical because everyone in the new center was a new employee.

The only thing that needed to be done was to translate the training into French and German and to evaluate any changes that needed to be made for cultural differences. The staff in India was also able to coach the staff in Poland on how to implement the Learning Path.

The idea of cultural changes reminds me of a funny story while working in India. The call center handled renting trucks for Americans who wanted to move their apartments or houses. Most of the agents didn't have a clear understanding of what is like for an American to pack up and move. They weren't aware of and were often surprised about how much stuff American's have, where they move, why they move and who is going to help them. So as part of their Learning Path, we spent a lot of time on just understanding America. One of the modules was called "Moving Day" and describe a move from one end to another.

I worked on another project where a manufacturing company purchased a factory in China to serve the Chinese market. Because of the weight of the finished project, it made more sense to make the product close to where it was going to be used.

The company had spent a lot of time rationalizing all their processes, creating standard work documents and building Learning Paths. Again it was very straightforward to translate all the documents, adjust for cultural differences, and training coaches and mentors. This was a very smooth process because everything was thought out in advance and training wasn't an afterthought.

Learning Paths will provide a forum and a process for handling the key challenges when two organizations come together, or there is major organizational change. First and foremost it takes off the table the discussion of how to proceed. It's a common model that everyone can understand and follow.

Start by selecting a Learning Path team that accounts for all the key stakeholders and creates engagement for those who will need to support the outcome. The process of building drafts of proficiency definitions and Learning Paths sets the stage for a great deal of interactive discussion. It helps get agreement on the obvious and finding the 80% that everyone can get on board with. Remember you are looking for both ownership and consensus.

In addition, by having a strong project champion, decisions can be made quickly, and resources get allocated in time. A good project champion also pushes the process along to try to overcome all the natural resistance to the change.

Engagement

There are always challenges you will face. Some of the people you need are on their way out the door and yet have the organizational knowledge and expertise you will need. HR needs to find a way to compensate and motivate these people to stay involved.

This challenge becomes magnified because the organization usually waits too long before trying to capture their organizational knowledge and expertise. If they have been building Learning Paths all along, they would already have what they need.

There are many instances that I've seen where an organization offers early retirement as a way of downsizing without any plan to capture what these employees know. Usually what they know is what to do when things go wrong.

In any event, Learning Paths becomes a process to get as much as you possibly can. It's a starting point for continuing to document and teach everything that historically been done.

In building a Learning Path, it's also a good idea to look at culture and values to see how to mitigate any conflict. If there are two sales organizations, there are usually differences in how they sell and how they treat customers. This is something that should be settled by the training department. This is the responsibility of senior sales executives. They have to determine the sales process, the sales goals, and the sales philosophy. The Learning Path describes how to teach people what's been decided.

I've seen organizations put off making decisions like these for weeks, months or years. As a result, the decision gets made by default usually by the frontline staff. In other words, the agent in the call center is now making corporate policy.

The secret of effective training for major organizational changes is to start early and adopt a process that can be replicated for each and every job. Ideally, at the start, there should be a high-level discussion about what it's really going to take to make the change successful. This is actually very similar to the discussion earlier in the book about adopting new technology.

CHAPTER 19

What's the Association?

Associations often have a mission or an obligation to provide educational opportunities for their members. This includes workshops, webinars, e-learning, discussion centers, and more. Associations also serve as collection points for a mountain of information including books, articles, podcasts, and whitepapers. Some associations even provide certification programs and competency models for various positions.

I've even been involved with associations that had a mission to recruit new college graduates to go into the industry and be ready to go to work on day one. This is usually an ambitious partnership with a college or university.

For the most part, professional associations are wonderful resources for information and training. There are two key issues that Learning Paths can address for these associations. First, there is often so much information and training that it's difficult to decide what to use and where to start. Just looking at all the articles there could be more than 1,000 to choose from. A course catalog from a convention might have more than 100 offerings.

Second, everything is designed for the entire audience. It's not company specific and sometimes not job specific. In an association that has 2,000 members, they aren't going to provide 2,000 versions of everything. So there is always the issue of transferring any learning to the job.

Let me give you an example of an association using Learning Paths to address these issues and serve members. Every industry has salespeople, so let's start there. To add some complexity, we will assume these sales-people need to be licensed and recertified every year. This is common in industries such as insurance, financial advisors, and real estate.

Best Practices

The first step is to get a team together to work on a Learning Path for sales-people. This can be for new salespeople, experienced salespeople, or both. On the team should be representatives from a handful of members who are viewed by the membership as practice leaders or thought leaders. If these people endorse and use the Learning Path others will quickly follow. This also ensures that everything is on target and up-to-date.

The team starts by creating a proficiency definition. Numbers such as sales volume or profitability will vary by member organizations so they may be left out or space may be left in for each member to customize the definition.

The next step is to map out a Learning Path. For new salespeople, assume the path starts the day after all the new hire paperwork and orientation is completed. Then using a calendar view layout teaching a generic sales process along with a series of joint calls that focus on each step of the process. This process might include creating a prospect, calling for appointments, initial presentations, closing calls, and follow-up calls.

Members can modify or replace this process if they have bought into a specific sales system or use different terms. They can also start with the generic process and then replace it later. Putting everything related to the sales process with all the coaching and experience is the goal.

The next step is to put industry- and produce-related training on the path where it makes the most sense. This is where the archives of the association come into play. The experts in the association know what they have and where it makes the most sense on the path. This same process can also be done if there are sales classes and workshops.

There should also be space left for company-specific training and information. This might include a company orientation or tour, or visits to select customers.

Some of the learning activities will be a discussion with experts. The association should have information or even e-learning that will provide useful content for these discussions. Links to specific articles, website, or courses can be added to the activity descriptions to help the expert guide the discussions. For example, read this article from the association site, and then we will discuss it.

Using an online system such as a learning activities manager will help organize and provide each access to all of these links. The end result is that you have integrated what the experts think with the resources of the association and the membership.

Back to annual certification for a second. Most licensing or certification requires a certain number of continuing education credits (CEUs). What typically happens is that at the end of the year, salespeople scramble for these credits and sign up for these courses at the last minute. Often they are looking for the ones that are easiest to complete rather than what might really help them.

A better idea is to start with an activity in the Learning Path that introduces a year-long plan for recertification. The experts determine which courses will be the most useful for our new salesperson and then determines when they should be completed. This is a prescriptive method rather than a "pick and choose method."

Learning Paths do rely heavily on coaching or mentoring. Many organizations may not have the time, resources or will to do this coaching. Since being in the association is voluntary, you can't force them to do anything. Some alternatives can be done through social media and networking. One idea is to set up peer coaching where small groups of salespeople meet on a regular basis by web conference to discuss issues and challenges as well as share success stories. Discussion boards or buddy systems are also good ideas.

Learning Paths are always mapped out in an "if I ran the world" format. Then when things happen you go to plan B or plan C. You make adjustments rather than mapping out multiple paths. As my friend Ira Kasdan, who is now sunning himself on the beach, always use to say, "Take the question of if off the table and focus on the question of how. We are going to get it down we just need to be creative in how we do it."

To sell the Learning Path to the membership, try piloting it with you thought leaders on the team. Their experience and advocacy will make a big difference.

Remote Workforce

Let's take a different tack to examine some possibilities where one of the positions is to make in-home service calls this might be installing water heaters or repairing appliances such as a dishwasher. The Learning Path can be built around each of the service calls and order them from simple to complex. The association can then provide instruction on how to do specific repairs on these calls. Having an instruction manual and a video will really help.

Added to the path can be a series of joint service calls to provide the experience and practice. When the new employee was flying solo, activities can also be structured where they take pictures or video of completed work as well as capture all the required paperwork. This can all then be combined and evaluated for final certification.

In both these cases, the association is maximizing their pool of resources and expertise of their thought leaders to provide something most of their members couldn't possibly come up with on their own.

Job Readiness

A final scenario deals with pre-hire training to provide new employees who are ready to go to work and make a contribution. The railroad example is a really good one. Again this was a project with several large railroads, a technical college, and Minnesota Job Skills.

The first step was to identify what prospective employees needed to prove what they could do before day one on the job. The job of railroad conductor is physically demanding, takes place out in the elements and can be potentially dangerous. If you're not paying attention to what you were doing, it's easy to get hit by a train or fall off a railcar.

As a result, the first thing was to provide an opportunity to determine if the student could and wanted to become a conductor. Fortunately, the railroads had donated to the college enough cars and track to simulate day-to-day activities. The students would spend a few hours in the classroom focusing on a concept and then go out into the practice yard and give it a try. If the class was held in the summer, they would work in the heat and humidity. In the winter, they would hold classes even if there was a blizzard.

Most of the class was spent on safety rules and regulations. There are hundreds of these. This included things such as hooking and unhooking cars, proper signaling, and use of the radio. Some of the students would self-select out of the class when they realized what the job was, but the ones who remained became very valuable to the railroads.

As a final note, associations have the potential for going well beyond their current education mission to help members get their employees up to speed and produce a lot sooner. It also encourages them to use the resources of the association rather than going through the time and expense of doing everything on their own.

CHAPTER 20:

Final Note

A Foundation

Where does the Learning Paths journey go from here? Learning Paths is built on a very solid foundation and a few universal truths that I don't see changing anytime soon. Of course, there are opportunities for making Learning Paths easier, faster, and more robust through technology and better measurement.

The foundation is the three learning principles presented in this book. The first is that learning is a process, not an event. It takes time to develop a higher level of performance and make any new learning second nature.

Second and perhaps the most challenging for traditional training is that knowing and doing are not the same. In fact, knowing and doing are very, very different. The search for faster and faster knowledge acquisition often misses the need to figure out how to put all that knowledge to work. Knowledge management is extremely valuable, but it's not the end goal.

Finally, principle three states that training should be by design and not by accident. With all the focus on informal learning and on-the-job training, it's important that it has to go beyond just assigning a learner to an expert or hoping through experience and practice everything works out. The fastest way to shrink the mystery period is to structure all that informal learning.

In addition to the three principles, there are also universal truths. No one becomes truly proficient without considerable practice and experience. Also, there is a real, measurable benefit for reducing time to proficiency. This is important because I think business will always value a strong business case for training initiatives.

When I think about those things that won't easily change, it reminds me of a newspaper headline from the future from the movie *Sleeper*. It read, "30 Year Study Reveals that Diet and Exercise Are the Best Way to Lose Weight."

I also think that there is a built-in resistance to moving away from the traditional school model that many businesses favor. Primarily, there always seems to be a safety in sticking to the old ways. It's worked so well for so many years. Well, it actually hasn't.

The advantage Learning Paths has in changing this paradigm is that Learning Paths is built on most people's experience in how they learned to get good at things. It's intuitive. Moving to what's easier for students versus what's easiest for teachers does make a lot of sense.

What does the future hold for Learning Paths? One of the biggest challenges will be to rapidly incorporate new technologies to improve training delivery, analysis, and reporting of results and managing the interactions including social media.

The Future

What I see in the future for Learning Paths is not this vast landscape of pick and choose options with massive databases of knowledge. Instead, I see rigorous structure Learning Paths that guide learners through the fastest path through the maze of options. Learning Paths will be linked to websites, blogs, videos, e-learning course and more that are delivered just-in-time and at the right time.

Technology is also going to make it easier to schedule, track and assess all of the informal interactions between coaches and learners. The tracking of all this information will also make it much easier to upgrade and improve training.

Finally, I think there is going to be much tighter integration between learning and enterprise-wide systems. This will allow the learning organization to become a more strategic player as organizations plan ahead.

Reviews

As I was writing this book, I asked learning experts and practitioners to read the manuscript and give me feedback. Some common questions came up that I would like to answer here. First, they would ask me about whether Learning Paths could apply for different jobs and different industries. My quick response was that it only applies to people. If a company doesn't have any people, Learning Paths doesn't work. Perhaps a better answer was to show them a short list of some of the jobs that have used Learning Paths.

Manufacturing Operators

- Fiber Cement
- Vinyl Siding
- Insulation
- Roofing
- Plumbing
- Corn Syrup
- Hydrogen
- Hydraulic Pumps and Equipment
- Paper and Packaging
- Metals
- Polymers
- Food Products
- Beer
- Paint
- Resins

Other Manufacturing Functions

- Quality
- Logistics
- Scheduling
- Maintenance
- Packaging
- Human Resources
- Procurement

Health Care

- Clinical Nursing Supervisors
- Home Health Aides
- Residential Health Aides
- Wound Care Physicians

Sales

- Construction Products
- Business Insurance
  - ✓ Property and Casualty
  - ✓ HR and Benefits
- Personal Insurance
  - ✓ Auto
  - ✓ Home
  - ✓ Life
  - ✓ Disability
- Business Travel Services
- Group and Meeting Travel
- Leisure Travel
- Consulting Services
- Truck Rental
- Trailer Leasing
- Vehicle Leasing
- Financial Services
- Sales Managers
- Furniture

Trainers

- Oil and Gas
- Personal Insurance
- Travel Agencies
- Financial Advisors

Newspaper

- Reports
- Editors
- Press Operators

Customer Service & Support

- Mortgage Loan Applications
- Credit Cards
- Travel Reservations
- Hotel Reservations
- Airline Reservations
- Mail Order Pharmacy
- Auto and Truck Fleet Support
  - ✓ Licensing
  - ✓ Billing
  - ✓ Rental
  - ✓ Compliance
  - ✓ Maintenance Management
  - ✓ Accounts Payable
- Construction Product Retail Support
- Business Travel Centers
- Rewards Fulfillment
- Debt Collections

Other Functions

- Railroad Conductors
- Portable Restroom Service Providers
- Firefighters
- Retail Merchants
- Senior Software Engineers
- Truck Mechanics

The second question involves using Learning Paths as a career path. Let's assume that you have a Learning Path for each function in your organization. Once you've established a sequence of jobs in a career path, you can align that path with a series of Learning Paths. The proficiency definitions for each Learning Path also provide guides on how to evaluate an employee's readiness for the next step.

A Learning Path is also a good source of information for employees about other positions. They can get a better idea about their readiness for those positions and if they really want to do them.

The third question revolves around the need for coaching and mentors to implement a Learning Path. This includes the selection process for these coaches and mentors. One answer is to create a Learning Path for coaches and mentors that spells out their required proficiencies and includes training on how to develop others. However, this is going to be a unique discussion in each organization based on existing resources and how management jobs are designed. Keep in mind that coaches and mentors don't have to be experts if other experts exist. In this case, the coaches and mentors guide the learning process instead of teaching it.

Summary

Learning Paths initiatives are a major change for most organizations. They take a sharp turn away from the traditional school model. On a positive note, a Learning Paths initiative closely mirrors other business process improvement approaches. As a result, a Learning Paths initiative is often more eagerly adapted at the business management level than at the training department level.

I've always found that the best approach to making this change is to start with a single function to prove the concept before rolling it out across the organization. This function should meet the following criteria:

- A large number of employees
- Customer facing or front-line production
- Championed by a senior executive

The last point is critical. Don't choose any function that doesn't have a committed project champion, the higher in the organization, the better.

I hope you've enjoyed this book and have found a few nuggets that you can apply immediately. I've tried to put as much of my thirty-plus years in training industry into this book. It's been an interesting journey.